ANNOTATED JAPANESE LITERARY GEMS

夏目漱石　富岡多恵子　井上靖

日本文学ルビ付き名作叢書

ANNOTATED JAPANESE LITERARY GEMS

Stories by
Natsume Sōseki
Tomioka Taeko
Inoue Yasushi

VOLUME TWO

Selected and edited by
Kyoko Selden

with Jolisa Gracewood
and Lili Selden

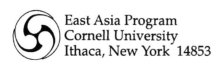
East Asia Program
Cornell University
Ithaca, New York 14853

The Cornell East Asia Series is published by the Cornell University East Asia Program (distinct from Cornell University Press). We publish affordably priced books on a variety of scholarly topics relating to East Asia as a service to the academic community and the general public. Standing orders, which provide for automatic notification and invoicing of each title in the series upon publication, are accepted.

If after review by internal and external readers a manuscript is accepted for publication, it is published on the basis of camera-ready copy provided by the volume author. Each author is thus responsible for any necessary copy-editing and for manuscript formatting. Address submission inquiries to CEAS Editorial Board, East Asia Program, Cornell University, Ithaca, New York 14853-7601.

Number 135 in the Cornell East Asia Series
Copyright © 2007 by Kyoko Selden, Jolisa Gracewood, and Lili Selden
All rights reserved
ISSN 1050-2955
ISBN: 978-1-933947-05-1 hc
ISBN: 978-1-933947-35-8 pb
ISBN: 978-1-933947-00-6 multivolume set
Library of Congress Control Number: 2006936584
Printed in the United States of America
24 23 22 21 20 19 18 17 16 15 14 13 12 11 10 07   9 8 7 6 5 4 3 2 1

Cover illustration from a Japanese stencil, late 19th or early 20th century, Herbert F. Johnson Museum of Art, Cornell University, gift of Drs. Lee and Constance Koppelman. Cover design by Karen K. Smith.

⊖ The paper in this book meets the requirements for permanence of ISO 9706:1994.

Contents

Annotated Japanese Literary Gems

Annotated Japanese Literary Gems makes available representative examples of short stories and novellas from Meiji to contemporary days. The series provides *rubi* for nearly all kanji at first use. Together with extensive annotations, it serves as a resource for students of modern Japanese literature and can be used as a text in modern Japanese.

Rubi is a printing term from "ruby," the English 5.5 point font, which is approximately the size of the small kana used here. The centuries-old convention of adding small kana to provide the pronunciation of kanji was widely practiced in modern printed texts beginning in Meiji. Japan's postwar Ministry of Education drastically reduced the number of kanji for official and general use and eliminated *rubi* from most publications.

The virtues of *rubi* are demonstrated by two recent examples. Yanase Naoki's translation of James Joyce's *Finnegans Wake* (I and II in 1997; expanded to I-IV in 2004) makes imaginative use of *rubi*, evoking late-Edo and early Meiji playful use of *rubi* as part of the exuberant word play that is present throughout the original work. In Senoo Kappa's autobiographical novel, *Shōnen H* (The Boy Called H, in two volumes, 1997), *rubi* makes the wartime episodes with obsolescent kanji compounds accessible to children and others of the postwar generations. In a brief note, Senoo explains why he used *rubi*: "In old books every kanji came with *rubi*, so [as a child] I was able to read adult books and learn kanji." Nowadays, children still pick up kanji from juvenile books with *rubi*. In the past, however, they effortlessly learned to recognize a vastly larger number of kanji from fiction and newspapers.

Rubi is invaluable in Japanese language learning. Looking up kanji and words can be fun, and it is important to develop kanji-Japanese and Japanese-Japanese dictionary skills. But constant dictionary work focused on single expressions not only slows readers but impedes their observation of other elements crucial to full comprehension of the text: how words are connected, how sentences are constructed, how the passage follows a train of thought, whose voice the line represents, and in what tone the piece is written. This series of annotated texts is intended to save heavy dictionary work and assist the reader to appreciate expressions in context rather than concentrating on kanji and vocabulary that are accessed elsewhere.

A small number of bilingual and annotated Japanese language textbooks already exist. Kodansha's Bilingual Books, which notably include *Key Words in the News* (1998), is one example. Annotated *rubi* editions of literary texts are rare, however. This series, with full *rubi* and informative annotations, may contribute to broadening the range of texts for intermediate to advanced Japanese students interested in language, literature, culture and society. In conceiving this series, inspiration was drawn from annotated language and literature texts used at the college level in Japan, as well as from similar European mini-volumes. As a rule, we combine two or three authors so that each volume introduces more than one theme, style, and level of linguistic challenge.

The text with *rubi* appears on the left and annotations on the right. Paragraphs (or passages where paragraphs are extremely brief) are numbered to facilitate locating annotations. A brief note on the author precedes each text. Abbreviations within the annotations are as follows: *no.* (note), *lit.* (literally), *hist.* (historical, history), *onomat.* (onomatopeia), *mod. J.* (modern Japanese), and *Ch.* (Chinese).

VOLUME TWO

This volume introduces one story each from three representative authors, Natsume Sōseki, Tomioka Taeko, and Inoue Yasushi. Natsume Sōseki, considered the greatest Meiji author along with Mori Ōgai, looked critically, often satirically, at Japan's "civilization" and examined human psychology, while also exploring literary styles. Tomioka Taeko began publishing poetry in the late 1950s before shifting to prose in the late 1970s. In fiction, she favors writing about nameless or unsuccessful, yet unusual, individuals with their peculiar fears and desires, illogicality and matter-of-factness. Inoue Yasushi, active from the late 1940s to the late 1970s, is acclaimed for historical narratives presented in stoic language, as well as for autobiographical fiction with a mild nostalgic tone. The selections from these authors represent ancient and modern scenes filtered through a Meiji mind, human drama in the late eighteenth century set in the vicinity of the Ise Shrine, and Japanese monastic life in eighth century Tang China.

I would like to thank Karen Brazell, Brett de Bary, Joan Piggott, and John Whitman for their encouragement and counsel over the years; Aguru Watanabe and Ryu Iwase for diligent word processing assistance in the pre-scanner days when this project began; Yoko Watanabe for preparing, as part of a directed reading course project, a brief, preliminary vocabulary list on Inoue Yasushi's story; students in Cornell University's Japanese reading courses for sharing my enthusiasm with these and other stories; and Karen Smith for professional editing, formatting guidance, and loving effort in preparing the cover design. The project was partially supported by the Consortium of Language Teaching and Learning directed by Peter Patrikis, to whom thanks are also due. More personally, Tsukamoto Tetsuzō's editing and annotating work on pre-Meiji Japanese literature, such as the prewar Yūhōdō Library and the postwar *tsūkai* (annotated) series, has long been a source of inspiration.

K. S.

夢十夜

夏目漱石

Dreams: Ten Nights

Natsume Sōseki

NATSUME SŌSEKI (1876-1916), né Kinnosuke, was the eighth and last child of Natsume Kohē Naokatsu and his wife Chie. Kohē was an influential town administrator and police chief of the late Edo period in Ushigome in the city of Edo. The household declined during the Meij era, and Kinnosuke was sent away immediately after birth to a family, then in the following year to the home of Shiobara Masanosuke and his wife Yasu, who formally adopted the infant. Kinnosuke was sent back and forth constantly between the Shiobaras and Natsumes, until he returned to his native home, still under the name Shiobara, following the Shiobaras' divorce. He lost his mother in 1881 when he was fourteen, and his two oldest brothers in 1887. In 1888, he was formally restored to the Natsume family, replacing his immediate older brother as heir.

Sōseki studied English literature with the intention of becoming a scholar. While at Tokyo University, he prepared a draft translation of Kamo no Chōmei's *Hōjōki* (1212; *tr.* An Account of My Hut, 1955) for his English teacher J. M. Dickson, and it was published under Dickson's name in *The Transactions of the Asiatic Society of Japan*. Sōseki was a classmate of the haiku poet Masaoka Shiki, and under his influence began composing haiku. The penname Sōseki, which he started using around this time, comes from an old Chinese tale about an obstinate man who mistakenly said "rinse the mouth with stone and use a stream as a pillow" (漱石枕流) (rendered in Japanese as "ishi ni kuchi susugi, nagare ni makurasu") instead of "use a stone as a pillow and rinse the mouth in a stream" (枕石漱流), and refused to admit the error.

Following graduation Sōseki taught successively at Tokyo Higher Normal School, Matsuyama Middle School in Ehime prefecture in Shikoku, and the Fifth Higher School in Kumamoto prefecture in Kyūshū. While teaching at the Higher Normal School, he practised Zen meditation at Engakuji in Kamakura, without, however, reaching enlightenment. Between 1900 and 1903, Sōseki studied in England as a Monbushō student. He is said to have experienced dismay at his linguistic inadequacy, especially of his spoken English, as well as from the gap between the literary principles of the West and the East. This apparently shattered his hopes of studying English literature alongside British scholars.

On returning to Japan, Sōseki took over from Lafcadio Hearn as teacher of English literature at the First High School and Tokyo University. He contributed haiku and *shaseibun* (literary sketches) to the haiku periodical *Hototogisu*, founded by Masaoka Shiki and later headed by Takahama Kyoshi.

This led to the publication, in the same periodical, of *Wagahai wa neko de aru* (1905-06; tr. *I Am a Cat*), a satire on Meiji's utilitarian society and a study of intellectuals who relied on that society. *Botchan* (1906), a story of an idealistic, short-tempered young Edoite who teaches briefly in a country town in Shikoku, is in part an affectionate caricature of Sōseki himself.

In 1907 he left Tokyo University to join the Asahi newspaper as a resident author. He began by serializing *Gubijinsō* (1907; tr. *Red Poppy*), *Kōfu* (1908; tr. *The Miner*), *Sanshirō* (1908), *Sorekara* (1909; tr. *And Then*), and *Mon* (1910, The Gate). These works handled unintended deception and extramarital love, among other themes.

In 1910, he collapsed with gastric ulcer while at Shuzenji spa in Izu. After recovery, he wrote *Higan sugi made* (1911; tr. *The Spring Equinox and Beyond*), *Kōjin* (1912-13; tr. *The Wayfarer*), *Kokoro* (1914). These were followed by the semi-autobiographical *Michikusa* (1915; tr. *Grass on the Wayside*), then the unfinished *Meian* (1916; tr. *Light and Darkness*).

In addition, he left short pieces like "Bunchō" (1908; tr. "Bunchō"), and "Eijitsu shōhin" (1910, Spring Day's Small Pieces). He also composed poems in the manner of classical Chinese poetry *(kanshi)*, lectured, and wrote critical articles about modern society.

"Yume jūya" (1920; *tr.* "Ten Nights of Deams") was first published in installments in the *Asahi* in 1908. In a concise, detached, and at times humorous style, the dreams reveal anxiety, guilt, fear, anticipation, and betrayed hopes.

SELECTED WORKS IN TRANSLATION

I Am a Cat (Wagahai wa neko de aru). Aiko Itō and Graeme Wilson, trs., Tuttle, 1972.

Botchan. Alan Turney, tr. Kodansha International, 1972.

The Miner (Kōfu). Jay Rubin, tr. Stanford University Press, 1988.

Sanshiro: A Novel (Sanshirō). Jay Rubin, tr. University of Washington Press, 1977.

And Then (Sorekara). Norma Moore Field, tr. Louisiana State University Press, 1978.

The Spring Equinox and Beyond (Higan sugi made). Kingo Ochiai and Sanford Goldstein, trs. Tuttle, 1985.

Wayfarer (Kōjin). Beongcheon Yu, tr. Putnam, [1982] 1967.

Kokoro: A Novel and Selected Essays (Kokoro). Edwin McClellan tr., essays translated by Jay Rubin. Madison Books, 1992.

The Three-Cornered World (Kusamakura). Alan Turney tr. Peter Owen, 1965.

Ten Nights of Dream, Hearing Things, The Heredity of Taste. Aiko Itō and Graeme Wilson, trs. Tuttle, 1974.

"Buncho" (Bunchō). Angela Yiu, tr. in *Michigan Quarterly Review*, Summer 2001.

This text is based on Iwanami's 1924-25 and 1993-99 editions of the Complete Works of Sōseki. In referring to the latter in annotations on Dreams 1, 3, 4, and 10, the date 1994 on the relevant volume is used. The original choice of kanji is honored, but re-produced in simplified postwar kanji form. Where other kanji preferences prevail today, they are indicated in parentheses following head-words. The postwar kanazukai is used throughout. All repeat symbols including ヽ, ゛ and 々 are reproduced in the text. Words with the multi-syllable repeat sign are written out in the annotation section as in きらきら because the symbol is hard to reproduce properly in horizontal writing.

第一夜

1. 腕組みをして [as I was sitting] with arms folded.　　枕元に (*lit.*) by the side of the pillow; by the bedside.　　仰向きに寝た who lay on her back.　　髪を枕に敷いて with her hair spread over the pillow.　　輪郭の柔らかな softly contoured.　　瓜実顔 oval face. From 瓜実, melon or squash seed.　　頬の底に beneath the skin of her cheeks.　　程よく差して gently tinged [with warm blood]; nicely ruddy.　　無論 naturally; of course.　　到底死にそうには見えない she hardly looks as if about to die.　　自分も確かに是れは死ぬなと思った clearly she is dying, I agreed. 自分 is used as the first-person pronoun throughout these dream pieces. Note, however, that the narrator refers to himself as 私 (わたし), not 自分, in conversation. The woman calls herself わたくし. 是れは (此れは in some editions) refers to the situation that be-comes the basis of a judgment: "this leads me to think"; "this surely means." 是 (れ) and 此 (れ) were common ways of writing the pronoun これ. The ending な in 死ぬな indicates affirmation: "I sense," "I feel."　　上から覗き込む様にして making as if to peer at her face from above.

夢十夜

第一夜

一

こんな夢を見た。

腕組をして枕元に坐って居ると、仰向きに寝た女が、静かな声でもう死にますと云う。女は長い髪を枕に敷いて、輪郭の柔らかな瓜実顔を其の中に横たえている。真白な頬の底に温かい血の色が程よく差して、唇の色は無論赤い。到底死にそうには見えない。然し女は静かな声で、もう死にますと判然云った。自分も確かに此れは死ぬなと思った。そこで、そうかね、もう死ぬのかね、と上から覗き

死にますとも "Of course I will die." とも indicates the speaker's strong conviction, usually in response to a question or a statement urging agreement.　潤のある眼 liquid/lustrous eyes.　只一面に all over; uniformly.　眸(瞳) the pupil of the eye; or, more generally, the eyes.

2. 透き徹る程深く見えるこの黒眼の色沢 the luster of these deep, limpid black eyes.　是でも死ぬのかと思った I wondered if she would still die [with eyes this lustrous].　ねんごろに politely; solicitously.　睜 (瞳、見張) ったまま with eyes wide open.　でも、死ぬんですもの、仕方がないわ "But I'm dying, there's no choice." もの follows an explanatory statement, often preceded by でも or だって, adding a note of protest or complaint.

3. 見えるかい "Can you see?" かい is an informal, masculine interrogative.　一心に聞くと when I asked single-mindedly / enthusiastically / emphatically.　見えるかいって、そら、そこに、写 (映) ってるじゃありませんか "Can I see your face, you ask, but look, it's reflected right here (in my eyes), don't you see?" *This is the woman repeating the man's question back to him, as part of her answer.*

4. 大きな真珠貝で穴を掘って dig a hole with a big mother-of-pearl shell [to bury me].　破片 （かけ, *alt.* はへん） fragment.　墓標 （はかじるし, *alt.* ぼひょう） grave marker.

5. 何時来るかね "When will you come?" かね is another informal, masculine interrogative.

5 夏目漱石

込む様にして聞いて見た。死にますとも、と云いながら、女はぱっちりと眼を開けた。大きな潤のある眼で、長い睫に包まれた中は、只一面に真黒であった。其の真黒な眸の奥に自分の姿が鮮に浮かんでいる。

自分は透き徹る程深く見える此の黒眼の色沢を眺めて、是でも死ぬのかと思った。それで、ねんごろに枕の傍へ口を附けて、死ぬんじゃなかろうね、大丈夫だろうね、と又聞き返した。すると女は黒い眼を眠そうに睜た儘、やっぱり静かな声で、でも、死ぬんですもの、仕方がないわと云った。

じゃ、私の顔が見えるかいと一心に聞くと、見えるかいって、そら、そこに、写ってるじゃありませんかと、にこりと笑って見せた。自分は黙って、顔を枕から離した。腕組をしながら、どうしても死ぬのかなと思った。

四
しばらくして、女が又こう云った。
「死んだら、埋めて下さい。大きな真珠貝で穴を掘って。そうして天から落ちて来る星の破片を墓標に置いて下さい。そうして墓の傍に待っていて下さい。又逢いに来ますから」
自分は何時逢いに来るかねと聞いた。
五
「日が出るでしょう。それから又日が沈むでしょう。それから又出るでしょう、そうしてまた沈むでしょう。——赤い日が東から西へと落ちて行くうちに、——あなた、待っていられますか」

6. 首肯た（頷いた）nodded; 首肯（しゅこう）.　　静かな調子を一段張り上げて raising her calm tone of voice by one level; raising her quiet voice a notch.　　思い切った声で in a resolute tone of voice.

7. ぼうっと崩れて来た [my clear image in her black eyes] started dissolving, becoming bleary.　　静かな水が動いて写る影を乱した様に as if still water moved, disturbing a reflection.　　流れ出したと思ったら the moment I saw [a teardrop] flow out [like water].　　ぱたりと *(mimesis)* with a sudden motion; ぱちりと, depending upon the edition.

8. 夫れから after that. 夫（れ）and 其（れ）were common ways of writing the pronoun それ.　　土をすくう度に each time I scooped dirt.　　貝の裏に [the moon shone on] the inner side of the shell.

9. 破片（more commonly pronounced はへん）fragment; かけ（欠）is the noun form of the verb 欠ける.　　かろく another form of かるく（軽く）.　　長い間大空を落ちている間に while falling through the vast sky for the longest time. *An effective, expressive use of* 落ちている, *suggesting the continued action of falling and the time it takes.* Cf. 大空から落ちてくる, comes falling from the big sky; 地面に落ちている, is found on the ground having fallen.　　角が取れて滑らかになった became smooth, its edges having worn off.

10. 苔 moss.　　是から from now on.

六　自分は黙って首肯た。女は静かな調子を一段張り上げて、「百年待っていて下さい」と思い切た声で云った。「百年私の墓の傍に坐って待っていて下さい。屹度逢いに来ますから」

七　自分は只待っていると答えた。すると、黒い眸のなかに鮮に見えた自分の姿が、ぼうっと崩れて来た。静かな水が動いて写る影を乱した様に、流れ出したと思ったら、女の眼がぱたりと閉じた。長い睫の間から涙が頬へ垂れた。──もう死んでいた。

八　自分は夫れから庭へ下りて真珠貝で穴を掘った。真珠貝は大きな滑かな縁の鋭どい貝であった。土をすくう度に、貝の裏に月の光が差してきら／＼した。湿った土の匂もした。穴はしばらくして掘れた。女を其の中に入れた。そうして柔らかい土を、上からそっと掛けた。掛ける毎に真珠貝の裏に月の光が差した。

九　それから星の破片の落ちたのを拾って来て、かろく土の上へ乗せた。星の破片は丸かった。長い間大空を落ちている間に、角が取れて滑かになったんだろうと思った。抱き上げて土の上へ置くうちに、自分の胸と手が少し暖くなった。

一〇　自分は苔の上に坐った。是から百年の間こうして待っているんだなと考えながら、腕組をして、丸い墓石を眺めていた。そのうちに、女の云った通り日が東から出た。大きな赤い日であった。それが

赤いまんまで（赤いままで）staying as red as ever.　のっと落ちて行った descended with an unexpected, abrupt motion. The mimesis のっと is usually applied to a motion of something large and conspicuous.　一つと自分は勘定した One, I counted.

11.　唐紅 "Chinese red"; crimson; vermillion.　天道 the sun.　のそりと slowly; sluggishly.

12.　勘定しても、勘定しても、しつくせない程 so many times that I could not finish counting no matter how often I counted.　苔の生えた moss-grown.　女に欺（騙）されたのではなかろうかと思い出した I began to wonder if I had been tricked by the woman. 思い出す often means "to recollect," but here it means "to begin thinking or feeling."

13.　すると then.　斜に diagonally.　青い茎 blue green stem.　見る間に before one's eyes; even as one watches.　と思うと the moment I saw that happen.　すらりと揺らぐ茎の頂に at the tip of the stem that swayed slenderly.　心持（心持ち）首を傾けていた細長い一輪の蕾 an oblong bud inclining its head somewhat.　ふっくらと (mimesis) gently. Used to describe something gentle and round (buds, cheeks, bread as it rises). Cf. ふくらむ.　瓣（花弁）petals of a flower.　真白な百合 pure white lily. This is suggestive of Easter lily, a symbol of resurrection. The editors of Iwanami's 1994 Sōseki zenshū points out that lily is also symbolic of purity and of Virgin Mary (vol. 12, p. 651).　骨に徹（応）えるほど匂った gave off a fragrance so intense that it penetrated to the bone.　遥の上から from far above.　ほたりと (onomat., mimesis) with a light, gentle flop; ぽたりと depending upon the edition. 自分の重みでふらふらと動いた [the flower] swayed with its own weight.　冷たい露の滴る、白い花瓣 the white petal from which cold dew dripped.　百合から顔を離す拍子に思わず、遠い空を見たら when my eyes caught sight of the distant sky as I lifted my face from the lily. 拍子 refers to musical beat, rhythm, or time, hence also chance or moment; 〜拍子に means "at the moment of 〜" and 思わず "unpremeditatedly."　暁の星 dawn star.

又女の云った通り、やがて西へ落ちた。赤いまんまで、のっと落ちて行った。一つと自分は勘定した。

又。

しばらくすると又唐紅の天道がのそりと上って来た。そうして黙って沈んで仕舞った。二つと又勘定をした。

一二
自分はこう云う風に一つ二つと勘定して行くうちに、赤い日をいくつ見たか分らない。勘定しても、勘定しても、しつくせない程赤い日が頭の上を通り越して行った。それでも百年がまだ来ない。仕舞には、苔の生えた丸い石を眺めて、自分は女に欺されたのではなかろうかと思い出した。

一三
すると石の下から斜に自分の方へ向いて青い茎が伸びて来た。見る間に長くなって、丁度自分の胸のあたり迄来て留まった。と思うと、すらりと揺ぐ茎の頂に、心持首を傾けていた細長い一輪の蕾が、ふっくらと瓣を開いた。真白な百合が鼻の先で骨に徹える程匂った。そこへ遥の上から、ほたりと露が落ちたので、花は自分の重みでふらふらと動いた。自分は首を前へ出して冷たい露の滴る、白い花瓣に接吻した。自分が百合から顔を離す拍子に思わず、遠い空を見たら、暁の星がたった一つ瞬いていた。

一四
「百年はもう来ていたんだな」と此の時始めて気が附いた。

第二夜

1. 和尚 priest.　廊下伝いに along the corridor.　行燈（行灯）（あんどう here, but more commonly あんどん）paper-covered lamp stand.　片膝を座蒲団（座布団）の上に突いて with one knee on a cushion [and the other drawn up].　燈心（灯心）を掻き立てた turned up the lamp wick.　丁子 tip of a wick; short for 丁子頭（ちょうじがしら、ちょうじあたま）/ 丁子花（ちょうじばな), so called because it resembles 丁子, a clove.　ぱたりと (*onomat.*) with a plop.　朱塗りの台 lamp stand painted vermillion-red. 朱（しゅ、あけ）is associated with red lacquer and, pronounced あけ, also the color of blood.　ぱっと (*mimesis*) suddenly; with a flare.

2. 襖の画 the painting on the screen door.　蕪村（与謝蕪村）Yosa Buson, painter and haiku poet (1716-1783).　～の筆 painted by ～.　黒い柳を濃く薄く、遠近とかいて、寒むそうな（寒そうな）漁夫が笠を傾けて土手の上を通る with willows drawn in ink, some dark and some light, far and near, with a seemingly chilled fisherman walking along the raised riverbank, his rain hat at an angle.　床 short for 床の間（とこのま), a recess in a room where a scroll can be hung.　海中文珠（海中文殊）の軸 a scroll painting of 文殊菩薩（もんじゅぼさつ, *Sansk.* Mañjuśrī), mounted on a lion, and crossing over the sea on a cloud. Mañjuśrī ("Glorious Gentle One") is the bodhisattva of wisdom.　焚き残した線香 incense sticks that have not burned out.　暗い方でいまだに臭っている were still giving off a scent in a darker corner of the room.　森閑として、人気がない hushed, without a hint of people. 天井に差す……丸い影 a round shadow (of the round lamp) projected onto the ceiling.　仰向く途端に the moment I looked up [at the ceiling].

3. 立膝（立て膝）をした儘（侭）while still with one knee drawn up.　左の手で座蒲団を捲って lifting one edge of the cushion with my left hand.　右を差し込んでみると as I reached underneath with my right [hand]. *The narrator feels for his short sword kept under the cushion.*　ちゃんと (*onomat.*) as expected; as appropriate. もとの如く直して putting [the cushion] in order as before.　どっかり坐る（座る）to plump down into a seat. The mimesis どっかり describes a quick, heavy motion.

4. お前は侍である you are a warrior. お前 in contemporary use indicates familiarity but in earlier times was a formal pronoun among the warrior class.　侍なら悟れぬ筈はなかろう if you are samurai, there is no reason why you cannot attain enlightenment.　そう何日（何時）までも悟れぬ所を以て見ると judging by the way you have so far failed to attain enlightenment.　～を以て with (an instrument), by (a method), through, on account of.　お前は侍ではあるまい you can't possibly be a samurai. まい is an auxiliary verb of negative conjecture or volition.　人間の屑じゃ you are the dregs of humanity. The ending じゃ（←である）is a variant of だ,

第二夜

こんな夢を見た。

和尚の室を退がって、廊下伝いに自分の部屋へ帰ると行燈がぼんやり点っている。片膝を座蒲団の上に突いて、燈心を掻き立てたとき、花の様な丁子がぱたりと朱塗の台に落ちた。同時に部屋がぱっと明かるくなった。

襖の画は蕪村の筆である。黒い柳を濃く薄く、遠近とかいて、寒むそうな漁夫が笠を傾けて土手の上を通る。床には海中文殊の軸が懸っている。焚き残した線香が暗い方でいまだに臭っている。広い寺だから森閑として、人気がない。黒い天井に差す丸行燈の丸い影が、仰向く途端に生きてる様に見えた。

立膝をした儘、左の手で座蒲団を捲って、右を差し込んで見ると、思った所に、ちゃんとあった。あれば安心だから、蒲団をもとの如く直して、其の上にどっかり坐った。

御前は侍である。侍なら悟れぬ筈はなかろうと和尚が云った。そう何日迄も悟れぬ所を以て見ると、御前は侍ではあるまいと云った。人間の屑じゃと云った。ははあ怒ったなと云って笑った。口惜しければ悟った証拠を持って来いと云ってぷいと向うをむいた。怪しからん。

now rare in standard Japanese.　ぷいと向こうをむいた looked away in a huff. The mimesis ぷいと describes an abrupt motion often characterized by lack of interest or displeasure.　ははあ怒ったな ahah, you're angry aren't you, [the monk said].　怪しからん not approvable; unpardonable; how impertinent; *the narrator's comment on the priest's speech and gesture.*

5. 刻（こく, *alt.* とき）hour.　悟った上で after reaching enlightenment.　入室（にゅうしつ; in Zen, にっしつ）する to enter a room; in Zen, to enter the master's room to receive teachings.　和尚の首と悟りと引替（引き替え）にしてやる I will take the priest's head in exchange for enlightenment. 〜してやる, usually a favor done downward, also indicates a vexed pose of wanting to get back at someone.

6. 自刃する to commit suicide with a blade.　奇麗に neatly; with determination; once for all; with no regrets.

7. 朱鞘の短刀を引き摺り出した pulled out the short sword in a vermillion-red sheath.　ぐっと柄を握って gripping the hilt firmly. ぐっと describes a sudden, resolute motion.　鞘を向こうへ払う to unsheathe a sword away from oneself with a sweeping motion.　一度に all at once; suddenly.　凄いものが手元から、すうすうと逃げて行く様に思われる it felt as though something horrific was escaping from my hand. 凄い dreadful; ghastly; amazing. すうすうと (*onomat./mimesis*) conveys a breezy, breathing, or hissing sound; also a smooth movement.　悉く切っ先へ集まって、殺気を一点に籠（込）めている all of it (the dreadful matter) gathered at the tip of the sword, a concentrated bloodthirstiness in one single point. 無念にも to one's mortification; regretfully.　九寸五分 standard short sword, because it measured 9.5 *sun*. One *sun* is approximately 3 centimeters (or 3.8 centimeters in traditional sewing).　已（止む）を得ず (*lit.*) without being able to stop; unavoidably; しかたなく.　已を得ず尖ってるのを見て seeing that [this sharp blade, reduced to the size of the needle tip to its mortification,] could not help but be pointed [at the end of its 9.5 *sun* length].　忽ち instantly.　ぐさりと遣り度（やりたく）なった felt like stabbing [with the blade]. ぐさりと (*mimesis*) describes a fast, plunging motion.　握っている柄がにちゃにちゃする the hilt in my hand felt sticky. にちゃにちゃ (*mimesis*) is used when something feels or sounds sticky, slimy, or greasy.

8. 右脇へ引きつけて置いて having pulled [the sword] close to my right side.　全伽（全跏）を組む to sit with legs crossed with the back of each foot on the thigh of the other leg; *kekka fuza* (結跏趺坐) in full. More informally, one uses *hanka fuza* (半跏趺坐), with just the right foot on the left thigh and the left foot under the right thigh.　趙

五　隣りの広間の床に据えてある置時計が次の刻を打つ迄には、屹度悟って見せる。悟った上で、今夜又入室する。そうして和尚の首と悟りと引替にしてやる。悟らなければ、和尚の命が取れない。どうしても悟らなければならない。自分は侍である。

六　もし悟れなければ自刃する。侍が辱められて、生きている訳には行かない。奇麗に死んで仕舞う。

七　こう考えた時、自分の手は又思わず布団の下へ這入った。そうして朱鞘の短刀を引き摺り出した。ぐっと柄を握って、赤い鞘を向へ払ったら、冷たい刃が、一度に暗い部屋で光った。凄いものが手元から、すうすうと逃げて行く様に思われる。そうして、悉く切先へ集まって、殺気を一点に籠めている。自分は此の鋭い刃が、無念にも針の頭の様に縮められて、九寸五分の先へ来て已を得ず尖ってるのを見て、忽ちぐさりと遣り度なった。身体の血が右の手首の方へ流れて来て、握っている柄がにちゃにちゃする。唇が顫えた。

八　短刀を鞘へ収めて右脇へ引きつけて置いて、それから全伽を組んだ。――趙州曰く無と。無とは何だ。糞坊主めと歯噛をした。

九　奥歯を強く咬み締めたので、鼻から熱い息が荒く出る。米噛が釣って痛い。眼は普通の倍も大きく開けてやった。

一〇　懸物が見える。行燈が見える。畳が見える。和尚の薬罐頭があり〱と見える。鰐口を開いて嘲笑っ

州曰く無と Zhaozhou said, "mu" (none, nothing; *Ch.* wu). This is a reference to the first of the 48 Zen *kōan* introduced with commentaries in 『無門関』(*Ch. Wumen-guan*; *J.* Mumonkan; "Gateless Gate"), written by 無門慧開 (*Ch.* Wumen Huikai; *J.* Mumon Ekai) in 1228 and published the following year. In Japan it was first published in 1291 and long remained popular. In the first *kōan*, in response to a question, "Does or does not a dog have Buddha nature?" Priest Zhaozhou answered in the negative. "Mu," nothingness, is a central theme in Zen Buddhism. *Wumen-guan* teaches that one cannot explain all by explaining nothingness.　無とは何だ。糞坊主め what do you mean by "mu," you wretched priest!　歯噛みをする to gnash one's teeth.

9. 奥歯 back teeth.　咬み締める to clench the teeth.　米噛（顳顬／蟀谷）が釣（痙／攣）って痛い I had a splitting pain in the temples. The expression こめかみ (*lit.* rice grain chewing) reflects the way one's temples (or more precisely the areas just under the borders of hair by the side of each ear) move when chewing food.　大きく開けてやった I opened [my eyes twice as wide as usual], so there! *The narrator's childish petulance highlights the hopelessness, or desperate hilarity, of his aspiration.*

10. ありありと vividly.　懸物（掛け物）scroll hung on the wall.　薬罐頭 "kettle-head," i.e., round, shaven/bald head.　鰐口を開いて his alligator mouth wide open. 鰐口 contemptuously describes a wide, flat mouth.　嘲笑った声まで聞こえる I could even hear his derisive laughter.　どうしてもあの薬罐を首にしなくてはならん no matter what, I have to behead that kettle-head priest. 首にする, (*lit.*) to turn someone into a decapitated head; hence, fire someone from work.　舌の根で念じた I chanted an invocation [to Nothingness] from the root of my tongue. 舌の根, the root or underside of the tongue, implies greater sincerity than 舌の先, the tip of the tongue.　無だと云うのにやっぱり線香の匂いがした even when it was obvious I wanted Nothingness, the fragrance of incense remained unchecked.　何だ線香の癖に how dare those mere incense sticks!

11. 拳骨を固めて making a tight fist.　いやと云う程 with all my might.　擲る（殴る／撲る）to pound, punch, hit.　（歯を）ぎりぎりと噛む to gnash or grind one's teeth.　膝の接目（継ぎ目）the joints of the knees; usually 膝の関節（かんせつ）.　どうあるものか (*lit.*) what is the consequence; i.e., who cares?　腹が立つ to be angered or offended.　ほろほろ (*mimesis*) in drops; also describes the way a pheasant sings.　めちゃめちゃにくだく to break into fragments; smash to pieces.

12. 凝っと坐っていた I sat still without budging.　堪えがたい程 unbearably. 切ないものを胸に盛（入）れて holding something painful in the chest. 盛る here

た声まで聞える。怪しからん坊主だ。どうしてもあの薬罐を首にしなくてはならん。悟ってやる。無だ、無だと舌の根で念じた。無だと云うのに矢っ張り線香の匂いがした。何だ線香の癖に。

一
自分はいきなり拳骨を固めて自分の頭をいやと云う程擲った。そうして奥歯をぎりぎりと噛んだ。両腋から汗が出る。脊中が棒の様になった。膝の接目が急に痛くなった。膝が折れたってどうあるものかと思った。けれども痛い。苦しい。無は中々出て来ない。出て来ると思うとすぐ痛くなる。腹が立つ。無念になる。非常に口惜しくなる。涙がほろほろ出る。一と思いに身を巨巌の上に打けて、骨も肉も滅茶々々に摧いて仕舞いたくなる。

二
それでも我慢して凝っと坐っていた。堪えがたい程切ないものを胸に盛れて忍んでいた。其の切ないものが身体中の筋肉を下から持上げて、毛穴から外へ吹き出ようと焦るけれども、何処も一面に塞がって、丸で出口がない様な残酷極まる状態であった。

三
其の内に頭が変になった。行燈も蕪村の画も、畳も、違棚も有って無い様な、無くって有る様に見えた。と云って無はちっとも現前しない。たゞ好加減に坐っていた様である。所へ忽然隣座敷の時計がチーンと鳴り始めた。はっと思った。右の手をすぐ短刀に掛けた。時計が二つ目をチーンと打った。

means "to allow in; put into. Cf. the usual reading of 盛 (セイ、もる) as in 盛大な儀式、料理を皿に盛 (も) る. The sentence says: "I endured almost unbearable pain lodged within my chest."　　筋肉 muscles.　　外へ吹き出ようと焦るけれども though [the painful thing] impatiently tried to spurt out [from my pores].　　どこも一面に塞がって……状態であった blocked on every side, it was as though there were no exit at all, an atrociously cruel state of affairs.

13. 有って無いような、無くって有るように見えた looked as though they were present yet absent, and absent yet present.　　現前する (in Buddhism) to appear before the eyes.　　ただ好い加減に坐っていたようである I seem to have been sitting there half-heartedly.　　所へ at that juncture.　　忽然 suddenly; abruptly.　　はっと思う to be startled; to start.

第三夜

1. 六つになる子供 a child who has turned six, who is six (*not* who will be six).　　を負ってる I am carrying [the child] on my back.　　慥 (確か) に自分の子である without question he is my own.　　何時の間にか before I realized it.　　眼が潰れて、青坊主になっている [the child] had gone blind and was shaven-headed. 青坊主 is a freshly shaven head or a person sporting one, like a novice monk. *The reference to the child's blindness and shaven head recalls Edo period itinerant blind performers and masseuses in monk's robes.*　　なに昔からさ oh, since no particular time; I've been blind since long ago.　　言葉つき the way he spoke; the tone of his voice.　　しかも対等だ moreover he spoke to me as a peer [not like a child speaking to an adult].

2. 青田 green rice paddies (around late July, well before the harvest season when the plant turns yellow).　　鷺の影が時々闇に差す the form of a heron flashed in the dark from time to time. 影 is anything that projects itself like a silhouette, form, light, a shadow, or a shade.　　「田圃へ掛かったね」と脊中で云った "We've come to the rice paddies, haven't we?" said the child on my back.　　顔を後ろへ振り向ける様にして turning my head slightly to the back.　　「だって鷺が鳴くじゃないか」 "But of course, because a heron calls."　　すると鷺が果して二声程鳴いた just then, as the child had said, the heron called twice or so.

3. 我子ながら although it was my own child.　　この先どうなるか分からない [if I kept such a thing on my back,] there was no knowing what would happen.　　どこか打遣る所はなかろうかと wondering if there might not be a place to dump the child.　　あすこ (あそこ) ならばと考え出す途端に the moment I began thinking that that spot might do.　　ふふん A derisive expression or a small, contemptuous

第三夜

こんな夢を見た。

六つになる子供を負ってる。慥に自分の子である。只不思議な事には何時の間にか眼が潰れて、青坊主になっている。自分が御前の眼は何時潰れたのかいと聞くと、なに昔からさと答えた。声は子供の声に相違ないが、言葉つきは丸で大人である。しかも対等だ。

左右は青田である。路は細い。鷺の影が時々闇に差す。

「田圃へ掛ったね」と脊中で云った。

「どうして解る」と顔を後ろへ振り向ける様にして聞いたら、

「だって鷺が鳴くじゃないか」と答えた。

すると鷺が果して二声程鳴いた。

自分は我子ながら少し怖くなった。こんなものを脊負っていては、この先どうなるか分らない。どこか打遣る所はなかろうかと向うを見ると闇の中に大きな森が見えた。あすこならばと考え出す途端に、脊中で、

「ふふん」と云う声がした。

laugh, implying "I know what you are up to."

4. 御父さん　おとっさん・おっかさん was still common in low town Tokyo in Meiji, before おとうさん・おかあさん (and the more formal おとうさま・おかあさま) became standard through the spread of kokugo textbooks.　「重かあない」(重くはない) "No, you aren't heavy."　「今に重くなるよ」 "Wait till I grow heavy." *This echoes legends about a man entrusted with a baby by a female stranger; the baby becomes heavy in his arms as he either waits for the woman's return or crosses a bridge with her.*

5. 森を目標 (めじるし, *alt.* もくひょう) に with the woods as my landmark/target. 田の中の路が不規則にうねって because the path amidst the paddies was winding irregularly　二股になった [the path] divided into two ways.　股の根 the root of the two-way fork.

6. 「石が立ってる筈だがな」 "A stone marker should be standing there."　小僧 boy; urchin; brat; (*originally*) priestling; errant boy.　成程 sure enough.　八寸角の石が腰程の高さに立っている a stone stood, 8-*sun* square and approximately hip-height.　表には左り日ヶ窪、右堀田原とある on the front it reads "Higakubo to the left, Hottahara to the right." Higakubo and Hottahara are actual place names in Tokyo.　闇だのに despite the fact that it was dark; 闇なのに.　井守の腹の様な色 the color like that of a newt's belly.

7. 闇の影を、高い空から自分等の頭の上へ拋げかけていた (the woods) threw a dark shadow over us from high above.　自分は一寸躊躇した I hesitated a little.

8. 腹の中では inside of me; in my mind.　よく盲目 (盲) の癖に何でも知ってるな he's blind, how can he know so much? めくら, now a discriminatory word, is replaced in current usage by 目の見えない人, 目の不自由な人, or 盲人 (もうじん).　一筋道 一本道, a single path.　「どうも盲目は不自由で不可いね」 "No matter how you look at it, being blind is so inconvenient," "Somehow being blind is quite inconvenient, you know."

「何を笑うんだ」

子供は返事をしなかった。只

「御父さん、重いかい」と聞いた。

「重かあない」と答えると

「今に重くなるよ」と云った。

自分は黙って森を目標にあるいて行った。田の中の路が不規則にうねって中々思う様に出られない。しばらくすると二股になった。自分は股の根に立って、一寸休んだ。

「石が立ってる筈だがな」と小僧が云った。

成程八寸角の石が腰程の高さに立っている。表には左り日ヶ窪、右堀田原とある。闇だのに赤い字が明かに見えた。赤い字は井守の腹の様な色であった。

「左が好いだろう」と小僧が命令した。左を見ると最先の森が闇の影を、高い空から自分等の頭の上へ抛げかけていた。自分は一寸躊躇した。

「遠慮しないでもいゝ」と小僧が又云った。自分は仕方なしに森の方へ歩き出した。腹の中では、よく盲目の癖に何でも知ってるなと考えながら一筋道を森へ近づいて来ると、脊中で、「どうも盲目は不自由で不可いね」と云った。

9. 「だから負ぶってやるから可いじゃないか」 "So I carry you on my back, what's the complaint?" 「負ぶって貰って　済まないが……親にまで馬鹿にされるから不可い」 "Thanks for carrying me, but somehow I'm not respected. Too bad I'm not respected even by my own parent."

10. 何だか厭になった Somehow I felt uncomfortable / fed up; I didn't like the sound of it. 「もう少し行くと解る。—丁度こんな晩だったかな」 "If you go a little further, you'll know—it was a night exactly like this, I recall." 独言の様に as if talking to himself. 「何が」 "What was?" 際どい声を出して my voice sounding nervous.

11. 「何がって、知ってるじゃないか」 "What, you ask, but you know what I'm talking about." 嘲る様に derisively; contemptuously. すると何だか知ってる様な気がし出した with that I started feeling as if I knew something. 分っては (分かっては) 大変だから since it would be awful if I found out [what it was]. 益 (益々) 足を早めた quickened my pace even more.

12. 殆んど夢中である I was almost desperate; I didn't quite know myself. 自分の過去、現在、未来を悉く照らして、寸分の事実も漏らさない鏡の様に光っている [the boy] illuminated every part of my past, present, and future, and shone like a mirror that left out not even the tiniest detail. *The paradox of physical sight and prophetic sight strongly recalls* Oedipus Rex, *in which the king is guided by a blind soothsayer to attain self-knowledge and blinds himself. In* King Lear, *Gloucester gains sight when blinded.* 自分は堪らなくなった I could no longer bear it.

13. 此所 Written 此処 depending upon the edition. 自分は覚えず留まった I stopped without thinking. 何時しか森の中へ這入っていた We had entered the forest before I realized it. 一間ばかり先にある黒いものは the black object about two meters ahead of us. (More precisely one *ken* corresponds to 1.82 meters.)

「だから負ぶってやるから可いじゃないか」

「負ぶって貰って済まないが、どうも人に馬鹿にされて不可い。親にまで馬鹿にされるから不可い」

何だか厭になった。早く森へ行って捨てて仕舞おうと思って急いだ。

「もう少し行くと解る。——丁度こんな晩だったな」と脊中で独言の様に云っている。

「何が」と際どい声を出して聞いた。

「何がって、知ってるじゃないか」と子供は嘲ける様に答えた。すると何だか知ってる様な気がし出した。けれども判然とは分らない。只こんな晩であった様に思える。そうしてもう少し行けば分る様に思える。分っては大変だから、分らないうちに早く捨てゝ仕舞って、安心しなくってはならない様に思える。自分は益足を早めた。

雨は最先から降っている。路はだんだん暗くなる。殆んど夢中である。ただ脊中に小さい小僧が食附いていて、その小僧が自分の過去、現在、未来を悉く照らして、寸分の事実も洩らさない鏡の様に光っている。しかもそれが自分の子である。そうして盲目である。自分は堪らなくなった。

「此所だ、此所だ。丁度其の杉の根の所だ」

雨の中で小僧の声は判然聞こえた。自分は覚えず留った。何時しか森の中へ這入っていた。一間ばかり先にある黒いものは慥に小僧の云う通り杉の木と見えた。

14. 文化五年辰年 the fifth year of the Bunka era and the year of the Dragon, i.e.,
1808. 丁度百年前 exactly one hundred years ago. *Sōseki was writing these dream
pieces in 1908.*

15. 此の言葉を聞くや否や no sooner did I hear these words than.... The phrase や
否や literally means "yes, or no?" 一人の盲目を殺したと云う自覚が忽然とし
て頭の中におこった the realization that I had killed a blind man came abruptly to
mind. *Legends about the sighted killing the sightless recur so that such wronging can
be felt as part of shared communal guilt memory. Some have associated this dream
with Kawatake Mokuami's successful kabuki play titled* Tsutamomiji Utsunoya-tōge
*(Crimson Ivy on the Utsunoya Pass, first performed in 1856). See Iwanami's 1994
Sōseki zenshū, vol. 12, p. 653.* 石地蔵 a stone image of Jizō. Jizō (*Sansk.*
Kṣitigarbha-bodhisattva) is a guardian deity of children and travellers.

第四夜

1. 土間 dirt floor. 涼み台 bench placed outdoors for cooling off on summer evenings. 床几 folding stool. 台は黒光りに光っている the bench shone with a
black lustre. 四角な膳を前に置いて with a square tray in front of him. 肴 dish
to go with the drinks. 煮しめ usually vegetables, but sometimes fish or meat,
cooked slowly in a soy-based soup till the liquid is nearly gone.

2. 酒の加減で due to the influence of sake. 加減, originally "addition and subtrac-
tion," can mean a grain of salt, a degree or extent, taste or seasoning, a state of health,
and so forth according to the context. 沢々して with a glow of health; more
commonly written 艶々. 皺と云う程のものはどこにも見当らない nothing that
could be called a wrinkle was found anywhere on his face; his face bore no wrinkles to
speak of. 白い髯をありたけ生やしているから (*lit.*) since he was growing as
much white beard as he could; owing to the profusion of white whiskers. There are
three kanji for ヒゲ: 髯 for whiskers; 髭 for moustache; 鬚 for beard. Here 髯
seems to stand for all three. ありたけ as much as there is. 子供ながら child
as I was.

「御父さん、其の杉の根の所だったね」

「うん、そうだ」と思わず答えて仕舞った。

「文化五年辰年だろう」

成程文化五年辰年らしく思われた。

「御前がおれを殺したのは今から丁度百年前だね」

自分は此の言葉を聞くや否や、今から百年前文化五年の辰年のこんな闇の晩に、此の杉の根で、一人の盲目を殺したと云う自覚が忽然として頭の中に起った。おれは人殺であったんだなと始めて気が附いた途端に、脊中の子が急に石地蔵の様に重くなった。

第四夜

広い土間の真中に涼み台の様なものを据えて、其周囲に小さい床几が並べてある。台は黒光りに光っている。

片隅には四角な膳を前に置いて爺さんが一人で酒を飲んでいる。肴は煮しめらしい。

爺さんは酒の加減で中々赤くなっている。其の上顔中沢々して皺と云う程のものはどこにも見当らない。只白い髯をありたけ生やしているから年寄と云う事丈は別る。自分は子供ながら、此の爺さ

此の爺さんの年は幾何なんだろう how old this old man might be. 幾何 (*Ch. jihe*) corresponds to the Japanese いくつ (how many); cf. 幾何 (キカ), geometry. Depending upon the edition, the kanji compound 幾歳 (*Ch. jisui*) is used instead of 幾何 and 幾年 below.　　筧 (かけひ、*alt.* かけい) bamboo water pipe.　　手桶 wooden bucket.　　神さん (上さん, pronounced - - - - with the rising accent) wife, usually of a merchant, store owner, artisan, etc.　　前垂 apron for wearing over kimono, rectangular and long enough to cover the knees.　　「御爺さんは幾年かね」 "How old are you, old man?"　　頬張った煮〆を呑み込んで swallowing the *nishime* that filled his mouth. 〆, or 締, is a symbol for "sealed."　　澄ましていた [the old man] remained unruffled; was composed; played innocent.　　拭いた手を、細い帯の間に挟んで thrusting her wiped fingers between her narrow sash and kimono.　　茶碗の様な大きなもので酒をぐいと飲んで gulping sake from a large vessel like a tea (or rice) bowl. ぐいと (*mimesis*) describes a motion with a jerk or a sudden pull / push.　　ふうと長い息を白い鬚の間から吹き出した exhaled a long breath through his white beard. 臍の奥 far inside the navel. *This suggests the womb.*

3. 河原 dry riverbed; river beach.

4. 瓢箪 gourd; container made of a hollowed and dried gourd for carrying water or sake.　　肩から四角な箱を腋の下へ釣るしている (吊している) [the old man] carried a square box under his arm, hung from his shoulder.　　浅黄 (浅葱) (*lit.*) the color of light onion green; light blue-green.　　股引 workmen's close-fitting trousers. 袖無し sleeveless top.　　足袋 socks with divided toes, normally made of cloth since the Edo period, but　before then also made of leather.

んの年は幾何なんだろうと思った。所へ裏の筧から手桶に水を汲んで来た神さんが、前垂で手を拭き

ながら、

「御爺さんは幾年かね」と聞いた。爺さんは頬張った煮〆を呑み込んで、

「幾年か忘れたよ」と澄ましていた。爺さんは拭いた手を、細い帯の間に挟んで横から爺さんの顔を

見て立っていた。爺さんは茶碗の様な大きなもので酒をぐいと飲んで、そうして、ふうと長い息を白

い髯の間から吹き出した。すると神さんが、

「御爺さんの家は何処かね」と云った。神さんは手を細い帯の間に突込んだ儘、

「臍の奥だよ」と云った。

「どこへ行くかね」と又聞いた。すると爺さんが、又茶碗の様な大きなもので熱い酒をぐいと飲んで

前の様な息をふうと吹いて、

「あっちへ行くよ」と云った。

「真直かい」と神さんが聞いた時、ふうと吹いた息が、障子を通り越して柳の下を抜けて、河原の

方へ真直に行った。

爺さんが表へ出た。自分も後から出た。爺さんの腰に小さい瓢箪がぶら下がっている。肩から四角

な箱を腋の下へ釣るしている。浅黄の股引を穿いて、浅黄の袖無しを着ている。足袋丈が黄色い。何

5.　腰から from his hip pocket.　　手拭 thin cotton towel, 30 by 114 centimeters or longer in the old days.　　肝心縒 originally 観世縒 (かんぜより), also 観世紙縒 (かんぜこより) or simply 紙縒 (こより), a narrow strip of rice paper twisted thread-thin and used for book-binding, etc.　　細長く縒った twisted till long and narrow.　　地面 (じびた here as a dialectal form of じべた; usual reading じめん) ground; じべた is the intended pronunciation depending upon the edition.　　しまいに lastly; in the end.　　真鍮で製 (拵) らえた made of brass.　　飴屋の笛 candy vendor's pipe. *Candy vendors used to make music to attract people.*

6.　見ておろう you will be watching; i.e., (*imperative*) keep watching. *Apparently there was such street entertainment in Meiji, and Terada Torahiko, scientist and essayist who was acquainted with Sōseki, mentions his childhood memory of one case. See Iwanami's 1994* Sōseki zenshū, *vol. 12, p. 653.*　　自分も見ていた I, too, was watching [the hand towel].　　一向 (一向に) (*with the negative*) not at all.

7.　ぴいぴい (*onomat.*) peep-peep; chirp-chirp.　　草鞋を爪立てる様に as if standing on tiptoe in his straw sandals.　　抜足をする様に as if taking stealthy steps. 手拭に遠慮をする様に as if keeping his distance from the towel.　　面白そうにも あった (面白そうでもあった) he seemed amused [as well as scared].

8.　ぴたりと已めた (止めた) [the old man] suddenly stopped his playing; the old man's playing stopped short. ぴたりと (*onomat.*) is when a situation or action is tight, exact, or sudden.　　手拭の首を、ちょいと撮 (摘、抓) んで、ほっと放り込んだ picked up the towel at one end and dropped it inside [the box]. Cf. 写真を撮 (と) る、 撮影 (さつえい). ぽっと instead of ほっと depending upon the edition.

9.　こうして置くと when I leave [the towel] this way; thus prepared.　　今に見せ てやる soon I'll show you; before long you'll see.　　柳の下を抜けて自分は蛇が見 たいから、細い道を何処までも追いて行った because I wanted to see the snake, I followed him along the narrow path as far as he went passing under a willow tree.

だか皮で作った足袋の様に見えた。

爺さんが真直に柳の下迄来た。柳の下に子供が三四人居た。爺さんは笑いながら腰から浅黄の手拭を出した。それを肝心綯の様に細長く綯った。そうして地面の真中に置いた。それから手拭の周囲に、大きな丸い輪を描いた。しまいに肩にかけた箱の中から真鍮で製らえた飴屋の笛を出した。

「今に其の手拭が蛇になるから、見て居ろう。見て居ろう」と繰返して云った。

子供は一生懸命に手拭を見て居た。自分も見て居た。

「見て居ろう、見て居ろう、好いか」と云いながら爺さんが笛を吹いて、輪の上をぐるぐる廻り出した。自分は手拭ばかり見ていた。けれども手拭は一向動かなかった。

爺さんは笛をぴいぴい吹いた。そうして輪の上を何遍も廻った。草鞋を爪立てる様に、抜足をする様に、手拭に遠慮をする様に、廻った。怖そうにも見えた。面白そうにもあった。

やがて爺さんは笛をぴたりと已めた。そうして、肩に掛けた箱の口を開けて、手拭の首を、ちょいと撮んで、ほっと放り込んだ。

「こうして置くと、箱の中で蛇になる。今に見せてやる。見せてやる」と云いながら、爺さんが真直に歩き出した。柳の下を抜けて、細い路を真直に下りて行った。自分は蛇が見たいから、細い道を何処までも追いて行った。爺さんは時々「今になる」と云ったり、「蛇になる」と云ったりして歩いて

仕舞には in the end.　　今になる、蛇になる、／屹度なる、笛が鳴る "Soon it'll turn, it'll turn into a snake / for sure it'll turn, the pipe will sound." なる (ー - with the falling accent) and 鳴る (- ー with the rising accent) are homonyms; their repetition creates a rhyming pattern.　　ざぶざぶ河の中へ遣入り出した (the old man) started to walk into the river, splish-splashing as he went.　　始めは膝位の深さであったが、段々腰から、胸の方まで水に浸って見えなくなる first the water was knee deep, but [the old man] became gradually submerged in the water from his hips to his chest, and then he could no longer be seen.　　深くなる、夜になる、／真直になる It'll turn deep, it'll turn into night, / it'll turn straight.　　頭巾 hood.

10. 向岸 （向こう岸） the opposite bank.　　蘆の鳴る所 where reeds rustled.

行く。仕舞には、

「今になる、蛇になる、

屹度なる、笛が鳴る、」

と唄いながら、とうとう河の岸へ出た。橋も舟もないから、此処で休んで箱の中の蛇を見せるだろうと思っていると、爺さんはざぶ／＼河の中へ這入り出した。始めは膝位の深さであったが、段々腰から、胸の方迄水に浸かって見えなくなる。それでも爺さんは

「深くなる、夜になる、

真直になる」

と唄いながら、どこ迄も真直に歩いて行った。そうして髯も顔も頭巾も丸で見えなくなって仕舞った。

自分は爺さんが向岸へ上がった時に、蛇を見せるだろうと思って、蘆の鳴る所に立って、たった一人何時迄も待っていた。けれども爺さんは、とう／＼上がって来なかった。

第五夜

1. 何でも余程古い事で I don't know for certain, but it was quite a long time ago. 神代 the age of the gods. 軍 (戦) battle. 運悪く by ill luck; unfortunately. 敗北た (敗けた) was defeated. 生擒になって captured alive. 引き据える to bring in and force [someone] to sit or crouch.

2. 脊 (背) が高い tall. 髯 (鬚) beard. 棒の様な剣を釣るして (吊して) いた wore a stick-like (i.e., straight) sword, slung [from his leather belt]. 剣 (ケン、つるぎ), the ancient double-bladed straight sword, was replaced in the Heian period by 太刀 (たち), the single-bladed slung sword with a slight curve. 藤蔓の太いの a thick wisteria vine. 漆も塗ってなければ磨きも掛けてない [the bows were] neither lacquered nor polished. 素朴な simple; artless.

3. 大将 military leader; captain; chief. 草の上へ突いて with [one end of the bow] butted against, or plunked into, the grass. 酒甕を伏せた様なもの an object resembling a wine cask turned upside down. 腰を掛けていた was seated. 鼻の上で、左右の眉が接続って (繋がって) いる his left and right eyebrows met above the bridge of his nose. 髪剃 (剃刀) razor.

4. 自分は虜だから、腰を掛ける訳には行かない since I was a captive, I was not allowed to sit on a stool. 胡坐をかいていた sat with legs crossed. 藁沓 straw boots. 膝頭まで来た [the boots] came up to my knees. その端の所は藁を少し編残して……飾りとしていた the custom was to fold over the unwoven straw ends [at the top of the boots] like a fringe, so that they rustled as one walked, to decorative effect.

5. 篝火で by the light of a bonfire. 篝火 is made with pine wood in an iron basket on a tripod. 捕虜にはだれでも一応はこう聞いたものである they used to ask this question of a prisoner no matter who he was.

第五夜

こんな夢を見た。

何でも余程古い事で、神代に近い昔と思われるが、自分が軍をして運悪く敗北た為に、生擒になっ

て、敵の大将の前に引き据えられた。

其の頃の人はみんな脊が高かった。そうして、みんな長い髭を生やしていた。革の帯を締めて、そ

れへ棒の様な剣を釣るしていた。弓は藤蔓の太いのを其の儘用いた様に見えた。漆も塗ってなければ

磨きも掛けてない。極めて素朴なものであった。

敵の大将は、弓の真中を右の手で握って、其弓を草の上へ突いて、酒甕を伏せた様なものゝ上に腰

を掛けていた。其顔を見ると、鼻の上で、左右の眉が接続っている。その頃髪剃と云うものは無論な

かった。

自分は虜だから、腰を掛ける訳には行かない。草の上に胡坐をかいていた。足には大きな藁沓を穿

いていた。此の時代の藁沓は深いものであった。立つと膝頭まで来た。其の端の所は藁を少し編残し

て、房の様に下げて、歩くとばらばら動く様にして、飾りとしていた。

大将は篝火で自分の顔を見て、死ぬか生きるかと聞いた。是れは其の頃の習慣で、捕虜にはだれで

降参する to surrender.　　屈服する to surrender; succumb.　　弓を向うへ抛げて throwing the bow away.　　するりと抜き掛けた began to unsheathe [the sword] with a smooth motion.　　それへ風に靡いた篝火が横から吹きつけた the bonfire wavering in the wind blew at it [the sword] from the side; buffeted by the wind, the flames blew toward the sword.　　楓の様に開いて opening [my right hand] like a maple leaf.　　掌を大将の方へ向けて、眼の上へ差し上げた raised it [my hand] above my eyes with the palm facing the captain.　　相図（合図）signal.　　かちやりと鞘に収めた [the captain] sheathed [his sword] with a click.

6. 其の頃でも恋はあった even in those [ancient] days there was love.　　一目思う女に逢いたい I wanted one [last] time to see the woman I loved.　　鶏が鳴く迄なら待つ I will wait if it's until the cocks crow; all you have is until the cocks crow. 逢わずに殺されてしまう I would be killed without seeing her.

7. 夜は段々更ける the night gradually advanced.

8. 崩れる to crumble; collapse.　　狼狽た（狼狽えた）様に in a fluster; in confusion. 焰が大将になだれかかる the flames seemed ready to crash down on the captain. Cf. なだれ（傾れ、雪崩れ、頹れ）snowslide; avalanche.　　誰やら someone not specific. 火がぱちぱちと鳴る the fire crackled.　　暗闇を弾き返す様な勇ましい音 a brave noise that seemed to thrust the darkness away.

9. 裏の楢の木に繋いである [a white horse] tied to a Japanese oak in the rear.　　鬣（髦）mane.　　高い脊にひらりと飛び乗った sprang up onto the tall horse's back. ひらりと (mimesis) indicates a swift, nimble motion.　　鞍もない鐙もない裸馬 a bare horse with neither saddle nor stirrups.　　太腹 big belly, usually of a horse.　　一散に駆け出した dashed off at top speed.

も一応はこう聞いたものである。生きると答えると降参した意味で、死ぬと云うと屈服しないと云う事になる。自分は一言死ぬと答えた。大将は草の上に突いていた弓を向うへ抛げて、腰に釣るした棒の様な剣をするりと抜き掛けた。それへ風に靡いた篝火が横から吹きつけた。自分は右の手を楓の様に開いて、掌を大将の方へ向けて、眼の上へ差し上げた。待てと云う相図である。大将は太い剣をかちゃりと鞘に収めた。

其の頃でも恋はあった。自分は死ぬ前に一目思う女に逢いたいと云った。大将は夜が明けて鶏が鳴く迄なら待つと云った。鶏が鳴く迄に女を此処へ呼ばなければならない。鶏が鳴いても女が来なければ、自分は逢わずに殺されて仕舞う。

大将は腰を掛けた儘、篝火を眺めている。自分は大きな藁沓を組み合わした侭、草の上で女を待っている。夜は段々更ける。

時々篝火が崩れる音がする。崩れる度に狼狽た様に焔が大将になだれかゝる。真黒な眉の下で、大将の眼がぴかゝと光っている。すると誰やら来て、新しい枝を沢山火の中へ抛げ込んで行く。しばらくすると、火がぱちゝと鳴る。暗闇を弾き返す様な勇ましい音であった。

此の時女は、裏の楢の木に繋いである、白い馬を引き出した。鬣を三度撫でて高い脊にひらりと飛び乗った。鞍もない鐙もない裸馬であった。長く白い足で、太腹を蹴ると、馬は一散に駆け出した。

篝りを継ぎ足した added more wood to the bonfire.　遠くの空が薄明るく見える the distant sky [above the bonfire] looked dimly light. *"Distant," because the camp is distant from the viewpoint of the horse and the woman.*　この明るいものを目懸て aiming at the brightness, the source of light.　しきりなしに incessantly.　蹄の音が宙で鳴る程早く（速く）so fast that the sound of the horse shoes rang in the air. 吹流しの様に闇の中に尾を曳いた (the woman's hair) trailed behind her in the dark like a streamer.

10. 真闇（真っ暗、真暗）な道の傍で by the side of the pitch-dark road.　身を空様に arching back.　両手に握った手綱をうんと控えた drew in the reins she held in both hands.　前足の蹄 the front horseshoes　発矢と（はっしと）(*mimesis/onomat.*) with a whack. It describes the way an arrow flies swiftly and hits the target, or the way a hard object like a sword or a spear strikes something hard.　刻み込む to carve or notch [the rock]. The horse chiseled the surface of the rock with its front horseshoes / drove its front horseshoes into the rock.

11. 緊めた手綱を一度に緩めた loosened all at once the tightly held reins.　馬は諸膝を折る the horse bent both its knees; fell on its front knees.　乗った人と共に真向へ前へのめった [the horse,] together with the rider, fell straight forward. 淵 deep water.

12. 鶏の鳴く真似をしたもの one who imitated the cock's crow.　天探女（天邪鬼、天の邪鬼）demon, as in folk tales and as seen under the feet of a guardian deity at a Buddhist temple. The name 天の邪鬼（あまのじゃく, *lit.* demon of heaven) is said to come from 天探女（あまのさぐめ）, a female god with a wicked heart.　此の蹄の痕の岩に刻みつけられている間 as long as the traces of these horseshoes remain carved into the rock.　敵（also 仇）foe.

第六夜

1. 運慶 (?-1223). Sculptor of the Kei School in the Kamakura period (1185-1333), based at the temple Kōfukuji in Nara. Son of Kōkei, colleague of Kaikei, and father of Tankei. Unkei's masculine, dynamic, and realistic style appealed to the warriors of the Kamakura period. He is particularly celebrated for the Dainichi Nyorai (*Sansk.*: Mahāvairocana) at Enjōji in Nara and the Kongō Rikishi (the Deva kings), with Kaikei, at the great south gate of Tōdaiji.　護国寺 a large temple in Bunkyō-ku, Tokyo and center of the Buzan branch of the Shingon Sect, founded in 1681 at the request of the fifth Tokugawa shōgun Tsunayoshi for his mother Keishō-In.　山門 temple gate. 仁王 the two Deva kings who are the guardian gods of the temple gate.　〜を刻む to carve.　評判 rumor.　散歩ながら while taking a walk; 散歩がてら.

誰かゞ篝りを継ぎ足したので、遠くの空が薄明るく見える。馬はこの明るいものを目懸て闇の中を跳んで来る。鼻から火の柱の様な息を二本出して飛んで来る。それでも女は細い足でしきりなしに馬の腹を蹴ている。馬は蹄の音が宙で鳴る程早く飛んで来る。女の髪は吹流しの様に闇の中に尾を曳いた。それでもまだ篝のある所迄来られない。

一〇　すると真闇な道の傍で、忽ちこけこっこうと云う鶏の声がした。女は身を空様に、両手に握った手綱をうんと控えた。馬は前足の蹄を硬い岩の上に発矢と刻み込んだ。

一一　こけこっこうと鶏がまた一声鳴いた。

女はあっと云って、緊めた手綱を一度に緩めた。馬は諸膝を折る。乗った人と共に真向に前へのめった。

一二　岩の下は深い淵であった。

蹄の跡はいまだに岩の上に残っている。鶏の鳴く真似をしたものは天探女である。此の蹄の痕の岩に刻みつけられている間、天探女は自分の敵である。

第六夜

一　運慶が護国寺の山門で仁王を刻んでいると云う評判だから、散歩ながら行って見ると、自分より先

しきりに repeatedly, intently.　　下馬評 gossip; irresponsible comment; advanced rumor. From 下馬先（げばさき）, a place to dismount such as before a shrine entrance, a temple gate, or a castle gate, and where servants gossip while waiting for the master.

2. 山門の前五六間の所には　10 or so yards from the front of the temple gate.　　赤松 Japanese red pine, grows to 40 meters and 1.5 meters in diameter.　　幹 trunk.　甍 roof tiles.　　松の緑と朱塗の門が互いに照り合って the green of the pine and the red-painted gate making a harmonious contrast.　　美事（見事）な beautiful.　その上松の位地（位置）が好い moreover, the placement of the pine was good.　　門の左の端を眼障にならない様に……突出している　[the pine] cuts diagonally across the left edge of the gate in ways that do not disturb the eye, spreading wider as it extends up to the roof.　　～とも思われる can be thought/understood to be ~.

3. 明治 1868-1912.　　車夫 rickshaw men.　　辻待をして退屈だから立っているに相違ない it must be that they are standing around [watching the sculptor] tired of sitting on the street waiting for a passenger. 辻 means crossroads.

4. 大きなもんだなあ it certainly is large. もん（もの）adds emphasis.　　余っ程骨が折れるだろう must be a lot more painstaking (than carving a human statue).

5.　へえ仁王だね I see, so it's one of the Deva kings.　　今でも仁王を彫るのかね so one sculpts a Deva king even today.　　私や又 (read わっしゃまた, from わしはまた) I just [assumed]. The man's speech here and in the following paragraph is in Edo dialect.

6. なんだってえますぜ (no pitch accent on な) according to what I hear; だってえます is a corrupt form from だといいます.　　誰が強いって when it comes to the question of who is strong.　　仁王程強い人あ（ひたあ, corrupt from ひとは）無いって云いますぜ it's been said that there's no man as strong as the Deva kings.　　日本武尊（やまとだけのみこと here, but more properly やまとたけるのみこと, "the valiant man of Yamato") a legendary hero and supposedly one of the sons of the ruler Keikō of the Yamato court, well known for expeditions beyond its territory to Kyūshū and northeastern Honshū.　　強いんだってえからね (corrupt from つよいのだっていうからね) for he's said to be even stronger [than Yamatotakeru].　　尻を端折って、帽子を被らずにいた he had the hem of his kimono tucked in his belt at the back and was hatless.　　余程無教育な男と見える he seemed pretty uneducated.

7. ～に委細頓着なく totally heedless of. 委細 by itself means "details," "the whole situation."　　鑿 chisel.　　槌 wooden hammer.　　一向 (with the negative) not at all.

にもう大勢集まって、しきりに下馬評をやっていた。

山門の前五六間の所には、大きな赤松があって、其幹が斜めに山門の甍を隠して、遠い青空まで伸びて居る。松の緑と朱塗の門が互いに照り合って美事に見える。その上松の位地が好い。門の左の端を眼障にならない様に、斜に切って行って、上になる程幅を広く屋根まで突出しているのが何となく古風である。鎌倉時代とも思われる。

所が見て居るものは、みんな自分と同じく、明治の人間である。其の中でも車夫が一番多い。辻待をして退屈だから立っているに相違ない。

「大きなもんだなあ」と云っている。

「人間を拵えるよりも余っ程骨が折れるだろう」とも云っている。

そうかと思うと、「へえ仁王だね。今でも仁王を彫るのかね。へえそうかね。私ゃ又仁王はみんな古いのばかりかと思ってた」と云った男がある。

「どうも強そうですね。なんだってえますぜ。昔から誰が強いって、仁王程強い人あ無いって云いますぜ。何でも日本武尊よりも強いんだってえからね」と話しかけた男もある。此の男は尻を端折って、帽子を被らずにいた。余程無教育な男と見える。

運慶は見物人の評判には委細頓着なく鑿と槌を動かしている。一向振り向きもしない。高い所に

振り向きもしない does not even turn around / pay attention.　彫り抜いて行く continued to carve out.

8.　烏帽子 black headgear men used to wear. In Unkei's time, aristocrats wore stiffly lacquered, tall *eboshi*, warriors wore shorter stiff *eboshi* with folds, while commoners continued to use the old-fashioned soft variety.　素袍 unlined, large-sleeved top garment, crossed kimono-like in front and tucked into the trousers; written also 素襖. 素袍だか何だか別らない大きな袖を脊中で括っている [Unkei] wore the large sleeves of his garment, whether a *suō* or what I could not tell, tucked in back [so they would not be in the way].　如何にも古くさい terribly old-fashioned.　わいわい 云ってる見物人 spectators who were noisily passing comments.　～と釣り合が取 れない (*lit.*) to be unable to keep in balance with ～; unbalanced; ill-matched.　今 時分迄 until this time; as late as now.　どうも不思議な事があるものだ how very odd; a strange phenomenon indeed.

9.　奇体 odd, rare.　頓と（とんと）(with the negative) not at all, まるで.　感じ 得ない 感じることができない.　仰向いて looking up.　自分の方を振り向い て turning around to face me.　流石は運慶だな this is just as might be expected of Unkei; so like Unkei. *The young man speaks like an educated man, with some self-satisfaction.*　眼中に我々なし (*lit.*) we do not exist in his eyes; he is heedless of us.　天下の英雄はただ仁王と我れとあるのみ (*lit.*) as far as heroes go, under heaven there are only the Deva kings and myself; the Deva kings and I are the only heroes in the world. Slightly archaic.　天晴れ admirable, praiseworthy; from あはれ (pronounced あわれ), moving.

10.　すかさず without a moment's delay.　～を見給え look at ～. 給え, from 給 う, to do a favor, is a friendly imperative used by men, now obsolescent.　大自在の 妙境に達している has reached the superb realm of absolute freedom. 大自在 is a Buddhist term referring to the ability to act as one likes yet without failing to benefit oneself and others, or a person who has that ability; another name for the Bodhisattva; also short for 大自在天, i.e., 摩醯修羅（まけいしゅら）(*Sansk.* Maheśvara), the pre-Buddhist Indian god who handled creation and destruction of all things and later came to be interpreted either as a guardian god or an opponent of Buddhism.

11.　太い眉を一寸の高さに横へ彫り抜いて (*lit.*) having horizontally carved out thick eyebrows one *sun* tall; i.e., the eyebrows are one *sun* thick.　鑿の歯を竪（縦） に返すや否や no sooner than he restored the blade of the chisel to a vertical position. 斜すに (so written to ensure the reading of はすに, but usually written 斜に; *alt.* な なめに) diagonally.　上から槌を打ち下した (*lit.*) struck a blow with the hammer

乗って、仁王の顔の辺をしきりに彫り抜いて行く。

八　運慶は頭に小さい烏帽子の様なものを乗せて、素袍だか何だか別らない大きな袖を脊中で括っている。其の様子が如何にも古くさい。わいわい云ってる見物人とは丸で釣り合が取れない様である。自分はどうして今時分迄運慶が生きているのかなと思った。どうも不思議な事があるものだと考えながら、矢張り立って見ていた。

九　然し運慶の方では不思議とも奇体とも頓と感じ得ない様子で一生懸命に彫っている。仰向いてこの態度を眺めて居た一人の若い男が、自分の方を振り向いて、

「流石は運慶だな。眼中に我々なしだ。天下の英雄はたゞ仁王と我れとあるのみと云う態度だ。天晴れだ」と云って賞め出した。

一〇　自分は此の言葉を面白いと思った。それで一寸若い男の方を見ると、若い男は、すかさず、

「あの鑿と槌の使い方を見給え。大自在の妙境に達している」と云った。

一一　運慶は今太い眉を一寸の高さに横へ彫り抜いて、竪に鑿の歯を返すや否や斜すに、上から槌を打ち下した。堅い木を一と刻みに削って、厚い木屑が槌の声に応じて飛んだと思ったら、小鼻のおっ開いた怒り鼻の側面が忽ち浮き上がって来た。其刀の入れ方が如何にも無遠慮であった。そうして少しも疑念を挟んで居らん様に見えた。

from above [the handle end of the chisel], i.e., drove the chisel diagonally down into the wood with a blow of the hammer.   一と刻みに削る to carve in one stroke. 木屑 chips or shavings of wood.   槌の声に応じて in response to the sound of the hammer.   小鼻 the wings of the nose.   おっ開いた widely open or apart; おっ開く *colloq.* from おし開く.   怒り鼻 "angry nose," a nose with flared nostrils. 其の刀の入れ方 his use of the blade.   如何にも無遠慮であった was quite unreserved; bold.   疑念を挟んでおらん様に見えた did not seem to have any doubts. おらん (from おらぬ) is synonymous with いない.

12. 能くああ無造作に鑿を使って、思う様な眉や鼻が出来るものだな how impressive that he can use his chisel so casually and still make the eyebrows and nose he wants; よく……ものだ is emphatic.   独言の様に as if talking to myself.

13. なに but no; a light negative interjection that indicates disagreement with a preceding speech.   あれは眉や鼻を鑿で作るんじゃない that does not mean sculpting the eyebrows and nose with a chisel.   鑿と槌の力で彫り出すまでだ all he does is carve out (the eyebrows and nose buried in the wood) with the power of the chisel and hammer.

14. 思い出した I began to think (*here, not* recalled).   果してそうなら if indeed that is so.

15. 金槌 iron hammer.   裏 the backyard.   先達っての暴風で倒れた樫を、薪にする積りで、木挽きに挽かせた手頃な奴 handy pieces from an oak that had fallen in a recent storm, which I had had a woodcutter cut up for me so I could use it as firewood. 暴風 is usually pronounced ぼうふう; 嵐 is the common kanji preference for あらし.

16. 勢いよく powerfully; energetically.   不幸にして unfortunately.   仁王は見当らなかった no Deva king was found.   運悪く unluckily.   彫り当る（当てる）to find / locate [the Deva king in the piece of wood] by carving.   三番目のにも仁王は居なかった nor was the Deva king in the third piece; 居なかった humorously personifies Niō.   片っ端から one after another.   仁王を蔵している [one that] held / concealed Niō within.   遂に明治の木には到底仁王は埋っていないものだと悟った I realized that Niō was never meant to be buried in Meiji wood at all. 遂に can mean either "at length" or "forever / till the end."   略 (also written 略々) more or less; for the most part; おおよそ、だいたい.

「能くあゝ無造作に鑿を使って、思う様な眉や鼻が出来るものだな」と自分はあんまり感心したから独言の様に言った。するとさっきの若い男が、

「なに、あれは眉や鼻を鑿で作るんじゃない。あの通りの眉や鼻が木の中に埋っているのを、鑿と槌の力で彫り出す迄だ。丸で土の中から石を掘り出す様なものだから決して間違う筈はない」と云った。

自分は此の時始めて彫刻とはそんなものかと思い出した。果してそうなら誰にでも出来る事だと思い出した。それで急に自分も仁王が彫ってみたくなったから見物をやめて早速家へ帰った。

道具箱から鑿と金槌を持ち出して、裏へ出て見ると、先達ての暴風で倒れた樫を、薪にする積りで、木挽きに挽かせた手頃な奴が、沢山積んであった。

自分は一番大きいのを選んで、勢いよく彫り始めて見たが、不幸にして、仁王は見当らなかった。其の次のにも運悪く彫り当る事が出来なかった。三番目のにも仁王は居なかった。自分は積んである薪を片っ端から彫って見たが、どれにもこれにも仁王を蔵しているのはなかった。遂に明治の木には到底仁王は埋っていないものだと悟った。それで運慶が今日迄生きている理由も略解った。

第七夜

1. 何でも (- - - - with the pitch accent on the first syllable) though I am not sure; according to what I think/hear. Used when the speaker is uncertain.　すこしの絶間なく same as すこしの絶え間もなく.　黒い煙を吐いて spitting black smoke. 浪を切って splitting the waves.　凄じい音である [the boat's engine] roars; makes a dreadful noise.　只 only; except that (also, free of charge); now usually written in hiragana.　焼火箸 red-hot tongs. 火ばし is a pair of iron chopsticks used for handling charcoal in the 火鉢（ひばち）.　帆柱 mast.　挂っている（掛かっている、 懸かっている）[the red sun] hangs [right above the tall mast].　仕舞には（終いに は／しまいには）in the end.　じゅっといって making a sizzling sound.　その 度に each time. そのたんびに is from そのたびに.　遠くの向うで far beyond.　蘇枋（蘇芳）の色に沸き返る [the blue waves] boil over in a dark / purplish red color. 蘇芳 is Indian redwood (or sappan), also a dye taken from its wood and bark.　その跡を追掛けて行く [the ship] follows in the wake of the sun [now set]. おっかける is a colloquial variant of おいかける.　決して追附かない cannot ever catch up [with the sun]. おっつかない is a colloquial variant of おいつかない.

2. 船の男を捕まえて catching hold of a crew member.　つらまえる (also written 捉まえる) is a variant of つかまえる.　怪訝な顔をして looking puzzled.　何故 （なぜ）, also read なにゆえ in formal writings.　落ちて行く日を追懸る様だから because we seem to be chasing after the setting sun.　呵々と笑った laughed aloud cheerfully. 呵々（呵呵）is also pronounced かか.

第七夜

一

何でも大きな船に乗っている。

此の船が毎日毎夜すこしの絶間なく黒い煙を吐いて浪を切って進んで行く。凄じい音である。けれども何処へ行くんだか分らない。只波の底から焼火箸の様な太陽が出る。それが高い帆柱の真上迄来てしばらく挂っているかと思うと、何時の間にか大きな船を追い越して、先へ行って仕舞う。そうして、仕舞には焼火箸の様にじゅっといって又波の底に沈んで行く。その度に蒼い波が遠くの向うで、蘇枋の色に沸き返る。すると船は凄じい音を立て>その跡を追掛けて行く。けれども決して追附かない。

二

ある時自分は、船の男を捕まえて聞いて見た。

「この船は西へ行くんですか」

船の男は怪訝な顔をして、しばらく自分を見て居たが、やがて、

「何故」と問い返した。

「落ちて行く日を追懸る様だから」

船の男は呵々と笑った。そうして向うの方へ行って仕舞った。

3. 「西へ行く日の、果は東か。それは本真か。東出る日の、御里は西か。それ
も本真か。身は波の上。楫枕。流せ流せ」 "The westering sun ends up in the east.
Is that true? The sun rising from the east has its home in the west. Is that also true? My
destiny is upon the waves, I know. The oar is my pillow. Row on, row on." 身, *lit.*
body, means one's person, personal situation, circumstances, course of life, destiny. 舵
枕, *lit.* oar-pillow, means sleeping on a boat, a boat voyage, synonymous with なみま
くら. 流す means to move or transport people or goods on water.　と囃している
boatmen were heard singing / chanting.　舳先 the bow or prow of a boat.　水夫が
大勢寄って、太い帆綱を手操っていた the crew members bunched together, hauling
in the thick cordage.

4. 心細くなった I began to feel uneasy / hopeless / forlorn.　何時 when (rather
than "at what hour," now written いつ in hiragana; another reading なんどき).　陸
is usually pronounced りく or (literary) くが.　何所 So here but written 何処
depending upon the edition.　慥か（確か）certain; now usually written たしか.
頗る very, quite.　際限もなく endlessly.　真白に泡を吹いていた [the waves]
were foaming white.　一層（いっそ）[would] rather; also いっそのこと. Used
when choosing a less undesirable option. Cf. 一層（いっそう）more; all the more.
身を投げて死んでしまおうかと思った I thought I would [rather] plunge to my
death [than stay on such a boat].

5. 乗合 passengers.　異人 foreigners (now obsolete).　欄 handrail, railing. Usually
written 手摺り; 欄 is pronounced ラン as in 欄干（らんかん, railing）. By itself,
欄 also means a column or section.　〜に倚り（寄り）かかって leaning on 〜.
半巾 handkerchief.　更紗 printed cotton, calico.

6. 甲板 deck.　天文学 astronomy.　死のうとさえ思っている I was thinking
even of killing myself.　天文学杯 such a thing as astronomy. 杯 is more commonly
written 等, and now usually など.　金牛宮の頂にある七星 the seven stars (the
Big Dipper) at the crown of the Bull.　自分に神を信仰するかと尋ねた asked me
if I believed in God.

7. 或時 once. Also 或る時; now only written ある時 or あるとき.　サローン
salon; lobby.　這入る to enter. This alternative way of writing (now obsolete) for
入る retains the original meaning of はいる from はいいる（written 這い入る or
這入る), to crawl in.　派出（派手）な衣裳 showy dress.　向うむきになって
with her back toward this way.　洋琴 Western koto, i.e., piano, as opposed to 和琴
（わごん）, Japanese koto. Cf. 提琴, "holding koto," i.e., violin; 風琴, "wind koto," i.e.,
accordion.　唱歌を唄う to sing, usually with instrumental accompaniment; now

（三）
「西へ行く日の、果は東か。それは本真か。東出る日の、御里は西か。それも本真か。身は波の上。楫枕。流せ〱」と囃している。舳先へ行って見たら、水夫が大勢寄って、太い帆綱を手繰っていた。

（四）
自分は大変心細くなった。何時陸へ上がれる事か分らない。そうして何所へ行くのだか知れない。只黒い煙を吐いて波を切って行く事丈は慥かである。其の波は頗る広いものであった。際限もなく蒼く見える。時には紫にもなった。只船の動く周囲丈は何時でも真白に泡を吹いていた。自分は大変心細かった。こんな船にいるより一層身を投げて死んで仕舞おうかと思った。

（五）
乗合は沢山居た。大抵は異人の様であった。然し色々な顔をしていた。空が曇って船が揺れた時、一人の女が欄に倚りかゝって、しきりに泣いていた。眼を拭く半巾の色が白く見えた。然し身体には更紗の様な洋服を着ていた。此女を見た時に、悲しいのは自分ばかりではないのだと気が附いた。

（六）
ある晩甲板の上に出て、一人で星を眺めていたら、一人の異人が来て、天文学を知ってるかと尋ねた。自分は詰らないから死のうとさえ思っている。天文学抔を知る必要がない。黙っていた。すると其の異人が金牛宮の頂にある七星の話を聞かせた。そうして星も海もみんな神の作ったものだと云った。最後に自分に神を信仰するかと尋ねた。自分は空を見て黙って居た。

（七）
或時サローンに這入ったら派出な衣裳を着た若い女が向うむきになって、洋琴を弾いていた。其の傍に脊の高い立派な男が立って、唱歌を唄っている。其口が大変大きく見えた。けれども二人は二人

more commonly 歌 (うた) を歌う. The word 唱歌 now usually refers to songs (in the Western scale) sung in elementary school music classes between early Meiji and 1941, when music as a school subject was called by that name.　其口が大変大きく見えた *This suggests Western singing with the mouth rounded, as opposed to traditional Japanese singing, in which lips are generally close together.*　丸で (with the negative) not at all; now always written まるで.　頓着 (とんじゃく, now more commonly とんちゃく) していない heedless; unconcerned.

8. 益 (also written 益々) all the more.　あたりに人の居ない時分 at an hour when nobody was around.　思い切って boldly; resolutely.　自分の足が甲板を離れて、船と縁が切れた其の刹那に right at the moment that my feet left the deck and my ties with the boat were cut.　命が惜くなった I held my life dear; I didn't want to die.　よせばよかったと思った I wished I hadn't done it.　厭でも応でも like it or not.　大変高く出来ていた船と見えて as the boat seemed to have very high sides.　足は容易に水に着かない my feet did not easily reach the water. 捕まえるものがない there was nothing to hold on to; there was nothing to catch me. 水に近附いて来る [I] gradually approached the water. *An effective use of* 〜て来る, *suggestive of the approaching moment when the feet will touch, as well as the water itself approaching the speaker.* 〜て来る *indicates the direction toward the speaker;* 〜て行く *indicates the direction away from the speaker.*　いくら足を縮めても no matter how much I drew in my legs.

9. 例の通り as before; as usual.　自分は……落ちて行った　Note the sentence structure:
   自分は　(the subject of 落ちていった)
   [(何処へ行くんだか判らない船でも……始めて悟りながら) while realizing that I should have stayed on the boat even though it was unclear where it was going,
   (しかも……出来ずに)] yet being unable to make use of that realization,
   (無限の後悔と恐怖とを抱いて) embracing endless remorse and fear
   (黒い波の方へ) toward the black waves
   静かに落ちて行った。I continued to fall silently.

第八夜

1. 床屋 barber shop.　敷居を跨ぐ to step over the doorsill, i.e., to enter.　白い着物を着て in white [barber's gowns].　かたまっていた who stood together.　入らっしゃい (いらっしゃい) a greeting of welcome; now usually いらっしゃいませ at stores.

以外の事には丸で頓着していない様子であった。船に乗っている事さえ忘れている様であった。

八
自分は益詰らなくなった。とうとう死ぬ事に決心した。それである晩、あたりに人の居ない時分、思い切って海の中へ飛び込んだ。所が——自分の足が甲板を離れて、船と縁が切れた其の刹那に、急に命が惜くなった。心の底からよせばよかったと思った。けれども、もう遅い。自分は厭でも応でも海の中へ這入らなければならない。只大変高く出来ていた船と見えて、身体は船を離れたけれども、足は容易に水に着かない。然し捕まえるものがないから、次第々々に水に近附いて来る。いくら足を縮めても近附いて来る。水の色は黒かった。

九
そのうち船は例の通り黒い煙を吐いて、通り過ぎて仕舞った。自分は何処へ行くんだか判らない船でも、矢っ張り乗って居る方がよかったと始めて悟りながら、しかも其の悟りを利用する事が出来ずに、無限の後悔と恐怖とを抱いて黒い波の方へ静かに落ちて行った。

第八夜

一
床屋の敷居を跨いだら、白い着物を着てかたまって居た三四人が、一度に入らっしゃいと云った。真中に立って見廻すと、四角な部屋である。窓が二方に開いて、残る二方に鏡が懸っている。鏡の

2. 窓が二方に開いて残る二方に鏡が懸っている there were windows on two sides and mirrors hung on the remaining two sides.　勘定する to count, 数える.

3. 其の一つ one of [the mirrors].　腰を卸した sat down.　御尻がぶくりと云った the seat of the chair made a bouncy noise [under my hips]; i.e., I sat down with an audible "plop."　余程坐り心地が良く出来た椅子 lit., chair constructed to be quite comfortable to sit in; quite a comfortable chair to sit in.　立派に映った (my face) was perfectly well reflected (in the mirror) / looked distinguished. りっぱ can refer either to the proper quality of the mirror or the proper appearance of the narrator's image.　帳場格子 a low two- or three-leaved lattice room divider placed close to the counter desk.　斜に diagonally.　往来 road; traffic.

4. 庄太郎 presumably a friend of the narrator; he appears again in the tenth dream. 何時の間にか before I knew it.　パナマの帽子 Panama hat, made of dried young leaves of jipijapa. In Japan it became popular around 1892.　女も何時の間に拵えたものやら I had no idea when he found a woman friend.　双方共 both [Shōtarō and his woman].　よく女の顔を見ようと思ううちに通り過ぎてしまった while I was trying to get a good look at the woman's face, they passed out of sight.

5. 豆腐屋 tōfu seller.　喇叭を吹いて blowing a bugle.　喇叭を口へ宛がっているんで since he was placing the bugle to his mouth.　頬ぺた cheeks.　蜂に螫された様に as if stung by a bee.　膨れたまんまで while [his cheeks] were still swollen.　気掛かりで堪らない I felt extremely concerned.　生涯 throughout one's life.

6. 御化粧 (おつくり, more commonly おけしょう) makeup.　島田の根 the root of the bun tied in back Shimada style.　島田 is short for 島田髷 (しまだまげ), a hairdo originating from courtesans at Shimada, one of the 53 stations on the Tōkaidō in Edo period.　何だか頭に締りがない somehow there was a lack of tautness about her head (hairdo); her hair looked somehow slovenly.　顔も寝ぼけている her face also looked sleepy / lacked focus.　色沢が気の毒な程悪い her complexion was so poor it made me feel sorry for her.　それで御辞儀をして、どうも何とかですと云った and she bowed [to someone] and said "how very something or other" [by way of greeting].　相手 the other person [the one the geisha greeted].

7. 鋏と櫛を持って with a pair of scissors and a comb in his hands.　自分の顔を眺め出した started to scrutinize my face.　薄い髭を捻って twisting my thin moustache.　どうだろう物になるだろうか what do you think, will it [my moustache] come to any good?; will I look decent enough?　白い男 the man in white.

数を勘定したら六つあった。

三　自分は其一つの前へ来て腰を卸した。すると御尻がぶくりと云った。余程坐り心地が良く出来た椅子である。鏡には自分の顔が立派に映った。顔の後には窓が見えた。それから帳場格子が斜に見えた。

格子の中には人がいなかった。窓の外を通る往来の人の腰から上がよく見えた。

四　庄太郎が女を連れて通る。庄太郎は何時の間にかパナマの帽子を被っている。女も何時の間に拵えたものやら。一寸解らない。双方共得意の様であった。よく女の顔を見ようと思ううちに通り過ぎて仕舞った。

五　豆腐屋が喇叭を吹いて通った。喇叭を口へ宛がっているんで、頬ぺたが蜂に螫された様に膨れていた。膨れたまんまで通り越したものだから、気掛かりで堪らない。生涯蜂に螫されている様に思う。

六　芸者が出た。まだ御化粧をしていない。島田の根が緩んで、何だか頭に締りがない。顔も寝ぼけている。色沢が気の毒な程悪い。それで御辞儀をして、どうも何かですと云ったが、相手はどうしても鏡の中へ出て来ない。

七　すると白い着物を着た大きな男が、自分の後ろへ来て、鋏と櫛を持って自分の顔を眺め出した。自分は薄い髭を捻って、どうだろう物になるだろうかと尋ねた。白い男は、何にも云わずに、手に持った琥珀色の櫛で軽く自分の頭を叩いた。

琥珀色の櫛で with the amber-colored comb [in his hand].　　軽く自分の頭を叩い
た tapped my head lightly. *The barber taps the narrator's head thinking that the narrator's concern was his hair.*

8.　さあ、頭もだが well, my hair too, but. *The narrator realizes that the barber's attention was on his hair rather than his moustache.*　　ちゃきちゃきと鋏を鳴らし
始めた [the barber] began making snip-snapping noises with his scissors.

9.　一つ残らず all, without leaving one.　　眼を睜（瞠、見張）っていた I kept my
eyes wide open.　　鋏の鳴るたんびに（たびに）each time the scissors made a noise.
旦那 a title (like "boss") to designate a male customer or a husband.　表の金魚売を御
覧なすったか Did you see the goldfish seller out front on the street? なすった is a
variant of なさった.

10.　自分は見ないと云った I answered I hadn't.　　それぎりで without further
ado; also それきりで、それっきりで.　　頻と again and again; enthusiastically.
危険 watch your step! The usual reading for these kanji is きけん; あぶねえ is
men's colloquial form from あぶない, common in Edo dialect.　　自転車の輪
bicycle wheel.　　人力の梶棒 shafts of a rickshaw.　　両手で自分の頭を押さえて
うんと横へ向けた [the barber] grasped my head with both hands and yanked it to the
side.

11.　栗餅 *mochi* made of millet, light yellow and sweet. "Awamochi ya, mochi yaa,
mochi ya" echoes typical sing-song vendor calls, some of which were still heard in the
1950's.　　と云う声がすぐ、そこでする [the *awamochi* seller's call] is heard from
right nearby.　　杵 pestle, pounder.　　わざと臼へ中てて deliberately hitting the
mortar [missing the millet dough].　　拍子を取って in beat; in rhythm.　　子供の時
に見たばかり I had seen [awamochi peddlers] during my childhood only; it was
childhood since I had seen them.

12.　あるたけの視力で with all the vision I had.　　鏡の角（かど、すみ）corner of
the mirror.　　帳場格子のうちに inside the lattice screen, i.e., at the cashier. The
screen is a low, folding room divider for the small front desk.　　色の浅黒い眉毛の濃
い大柄な女 somewhat dark-complexioned large woman with dark eyebrows.　　髪を
銀杏返しに結って in "butterfly" style, or literally a "gingko-leaf coiffure." 銀杏返
し, worn by young women in Edo period but mature women from Meiji on, is a style
with the bun in back split in two semi-circular shapes.　　黒繻子 black satin.　　半襟
"half collar," a collar cover to protect the part of the kimono collar around the neck and
in the front.

「さあ、頭もだが、どうだろう、物になるだろうか」と自分は白い男に聞いた。白い男は矢張り何も

答えずに、ちゃきちゃきと鋏を鳴らし始めた。

鏡に映る影を一つ残らず見る積りで眼を睜っていたが、鋏の鳴るたんびに黒い毛が飛んで来るので、

恐ろしくなって、やがて眼を閉じた。すると白い男が、こう云った。

「旦那は表の金魚売を御覧なすったか」

自分は見ないと云った。白い男はそれぎりで、頻と鋏を鳴らしていた。すると突然大きな声で危険

と云ったものがある。はっと眼を開けると、白い男の袖の下に自転車の輪が見えた。人力の梶棒が見

えた。と思うと、白い男が両手で自分の頭を押さえてうんと横へ向けた。自転車と人力車は丸で見え

なくなった。鋏の音がちゃきちゃきする。

やがて、白い男は自分の横へ廻って、耳の所を刈り始めた。毛が前の方へ飛ばなくなったから、安

心して眼を開けた。粟餅や、餅やあ、餅や、と云う声がすぐ、そこでする。小さい杵をわざと臼へ中

てて、拍子を取って餅を搗いている。粟餅屋は子供の時に見たばかりだから、一寸様子が見たい。け

れども粟餅屋は決して鏡の中に出て来ない。只餅を搗く音だけする。

自分はあるたけの視力で鏡の角を覗き込む様にして見た。すると帳場格子のうちに、いつの間にか

一人の女が坐っている。色の浅黒い眉毛の濃い大柄な女で、髪を銀杏返しに結って、黒儒子の半襟の

素袷 lined kimono worn by itself without an undergarment.　立膝の儘 with one knee drawn up.　札 bills; more commonly お札.　十円札 ten-yen bills.　長い睫を伏せて薄い唇を結んで with long eyelashes cast down and thin lips tightly pressed together.　どこまで行っても尽きる様子がない [the number of bills] never seemed to come to an end no matter how many she counted.　高々 at most.

13. 茫然として stunned; in a daze; absentmindedly.　洗いましょう let me now wash your hair.　丁度うまい折だから since this was a good chance.　立ち上がるや否や the moment I rose.

14. 代を払って after paying the fee.　門口 entrance　小判なりの桶が五つばかり five or so oval-shaped wooden basins. 小判 and 大判 respectively were small and large oval gold coins.　斑入りの speckled; motley; multi-colored.　頬杖を突いて resting his cheeks on his hands.　殆ど〜ない hardly.

掛った素裕で、立膝の儘、札の勘定をしている。札は十円札らしい。女は長い睫を伏せて薄い唇を結んで一生懸命に、札の数を読んでいるが、其の読み方がいかにも早い。しかも札の数はどこまで行っても尽きる様子がない。膝の上に乗っているのは高々百枚位だが、其の百枚がいつ迄勘定しても百枚である。

一三
　自分は茫然としてこの女の顔と十円札を見詰めて居た。すると耳の元で白い男が大きな声で「洗いましょう」と云った。丁度うまい折だから、椅子から立ち上がるや否や、帳場格子の方を振り返って見た。けれども格子のうちには女も札も何にも見えなかった。

一四
　代を払って表へ出ると、門口の左側に、小判なりの桶が五つ許り並べてあって、其の中に赤い金魚や、斑入りの金魚や、痩せた金魚や、肥った金魚が沢山入れてあった。そうして金魚売が其の後ろにいた。金魚売は自分の前に並べた金魚を見詰めた儘、頬杖を突いて、じっとして居る。騒がしい往来の活動には殆ど心を留めていない。自分はしばらく立って此の金魚売を眺めて居た。けれども自分が眺めている間、金魚売はちっとも動かなかった。

第九夜

1. 世の中 the world; society; the times.　　ざわつき始めた began to be noisy / restless.　　今にも……そうに [war seemed] ready to [break out] at any moment. 焼け出された裸馬 unsaddled horses burnt out of their stables.　　夜昼となく day and night.　　屋敷の周囲を around the houses.　　暴れ廻る to rage about; run about wildly. Now あれまわる for winds but usually あばれまわる for horses.　　足軽共 footmen. 足軽 is a samurai of the lowest rank.　　犇きながら jostling one another. それでいて and yet; even so.　　森として (*onomat.*) hushed.

2. 三つになる子供 a child in his third (calendar) year of age.　　草鞋 straw sandals. 黒い頭巾 black headwear [to conceal his identity].　　勝手口から through the kitchen / back door. This is to avoid the front entrance, where he may be spotted.　　雪 洞 paper lantern with a handle.　　暗い闇に細長く射して throwing a long light into the dark.　　生垣 hedge; live fence.　　檜 hinoki cypress; Japanese cypress; white cedar.

3. それきり (with the negative) never again. This was the last time they saw him. 御父様 This formal appellation suggests that the father is a middle to upper class samurai.　　「あっち」と答える様になった he learned to answer "that way."　　「何 日御帰り」 "When will he return?" 御帰り is short for お帰りになるの.　　何遍と なく over and over; countless times.　　「今に」だけを覚えたのみである he only learned to say "soon" and nothing else; the only answer he learned was "soon." だけ and のみ are synonymous but the latter is more formal.

4. 四隣 The kanji suggests "neighborhood on all four sides." Usually written あたり or 辺り.　　帯を締め直して retying her sash.　　鮫鞘の短刀 a dagger in a shark-skin mounted sheath.　　潜り side door; short for 潜り戸, smaller door for private use by the side of the main, often double-leafed, door.　　草鞋 straw sandals as opposed to *geta*, wooden clogs.

第九夜

世の中が何となくざわつき始めた。今にも戦争が起りそうに見える。焼け出された裸馬が、夜昼となく、屋敷の周囲を暴れ廻ると、それを夜昼となく足軽共が犇きながら追掛けている様な心持がする。それでいて家のうちは森として静かである。

家には若い母と三つになる子供がいる。父は何処かへ行った。父が何処かへ行ったのは、月の出ていない夜中であった。床の上で草鞋を穿いて、黒い頭巾を被って、勝手口から出て行った。其の時母の持っていた雪洞の灯が暗い闇に細長く射して、生垣の手前にある古い檜を照らした。

父はそれ限帰って来なかった。母は毎日三つになる子供に「御父様は」ときいている。子供は何とも云わなかった。しばらくしてから「あっち」と答える様になった。母が「何時御帰り」と聞いても矢張り「あっち」と答えて笑っていた。其の時は母も笑った。そうして「今に御帰り」と云う言葉を何遍となく繰返して教えた。けれども子供は「今に」丈を覚えたのみである。時々は「御父様は何処」と聞かれて「今に」と答える事もあった。

夜になって、四隣が静まると、母は帯を締め直して、鮫鞘の短刀を帯の間へ差して、子供を細帯で脊中へ脊負って、そっと潜りから出て行く。母はいつでも草鞋を穿いていた。子供は此の草鞋の音を

5. 土塀 mud walls; the pronunciation preference is つちべい depending upon the edition.　屋敷町 samurai residential area. 屋敷 is short for 武家屋敷, samurai houses.　だらだら坂 long downward slope.　降り尽くす to go all the way down. 銀杏 gingko tree.　〜を目標に with 〜 as the landmark.　右に切れる to turn to the right.　一丁ばかり奥に approximately 1 *chō* further along the road. One *chō* is nearly 120 yards.　鳥居 gate-like structure, usually of two beams and two pillars, marking the entrance to a shrine.　片側は田圃で、片側は熊笹ばかりの中を鳥居まで来て walking as far as to the *torii* along the path between rice paddies on one side and nothing else but bamboo grass on the other.　暗い杉の木立 rows of dark cedar trees. The path leading to a Shintō shrine is usually lined with cedar trees on both sides. 二十間ばかり approximately 40 yards. One *ken* is nearly 6 feet.　敷石伝いに突き当たると after following the pavement (or paving stones) all the way.　古い拝殿の階段の下 [one finds oneself] beneath the steps of an old worship hall.　鼠色に洗い出された賽銭箱 offertory box washed gray in the rain. The box at the front of the worship hall, made of unstained wood, turns gray as it ages.　大きな鈴の紐 a heavy bell rope [which hangs above the offertory box]. Visitors customarily clap their hands and tug on the rope before the worship hall.　八幡宮 Hachiman Shrine. A Hachiman shrine enshrines the guardian deity of warriors, i.e., the legendary Emperor Ōjin, flanked by his mother (known as Empress Jingū) and his spouse (Hime Ōkami) or son (Emperor Chūai).　額 tablet.　八の字が、鳩が二羽向いあった様な書体に出来ている the kanji 八 is made in a calligraphic style suggestive of two pigeons facing each other.　家中のもの some member of the Daimyō household, i.e., a retainer. 金的 the golden target, i.e., a one-centimeter bull's eye painted on a three-centimeter square gold color plate. An ordinary target being much larger, hitting the golden target meant great prestige.　偶には occasionally; on rare occasions.　太刀 an older type of sword slung from the waist, unlike the katana, which was thrust through the belt.

6. 梢 treetop.　梟 owl.　冷飯草履 plain straw sandals. 冷飯（冷や飯）, cold rice; 冷飯食（ひやめしくい）, *lit.*, eaters of cold rice; sons who were not heirs (in Edo period), hangers-on, or people treated coldly.　ぴちゃぴちゃ (*onomat.*) splashing; splattering; tip-tap; slop, slop.　已む（止む）to stop (v.i.).　柏手を打つ to clap one's hands in respect for the gods.　一心不乱に "with singleness of mind and without distraction"; wholeheartedly; with great concentration.　〜の無事を祈る to pray for the safety of 〜.　弓矢の神の八幡 the Hachiman god(s), guardian(s) of bows and arrows.　是非ない beyond any judgment; desperate.　願を掛ける to offer a prayer with a vow; pray for the fulfillment of one's wish.　よもや聴かれぬ道理はなかろうと that there was absolutely no reason why she would not be heard. よもや (with negative conjecture) not least likely.　一図に single-mindedly;

聞きながら母の脊中で寝て仕舞う事もあった。

五　土塀の続いている屋敷町を西へ下って、だらゝ坂を降り尽くすと、大きな銀杏がある。此の銀杏を目標に右に切れると、一丁ばかり奥に石の鳥居がある。片側は田圃で、片側は熊笹ばかりの中を鳥居迄来て、それを潜り抜けると、暗い杉の木立になる。それから二十間許り敷石伝いに突き当ると、古い拝殿の階段の下にでる。鼠色に洗い出された賽銭箱の上に、大きな鈴の紐がぶら下って昼間見ると、その鈴の傍に八幡宮と云う額が懸っている。八の字が、鳩が二羽向いあった様な書体に出来ているのが面白い。其の外にも色々の額がある。大抵は家中のものゝ射抜いた金的を、射抜いたものの名前に添えたのが多い。偶には太刀を納めたのもある。

六　鳥居を潜ると杉の梢で何時でも梟が鳴いている。そうして、冷飯草履の音がぴちゃぴちゃする。それが拝殿の前で已むと、母は先ず鈴を鳴らして置いて、直ぐにしゃがんで柏手を打つ。大抵は此の時梟が急に鳴かなくなる。それから母は一心不乱に夫の無事を祈る。母の考えでは、夫が侍であるから、弓矢の神の八幡へ、こうやって是非ない願を掛けたら、よもや聴かれぬ道理はなかろうと一図に思い詰めて居る。

七　子供は能く此の鈴の音で眼を覚まして、四辺を見ると真暗だものだから、急に脊中で泣き出す事がある。其の時母は口の内で何か祈りながら、脊を振ってあやそうとする。すると旨く泣き已む事もあ

whole-heartedly.　思い詰める to think intently.

7. 能く now usually written with hiragana only; can be written with 良, 善, 好, 宜, or 能 depending upon the meaning. 能 signifies potential (the child can / may wake), which also suggests frequency (the child sometimes / often wakes). 真暗だものだから since it is all dark, 真暗なものだから. 脊を振ってあやそうとする tries to pacify [the child] by shaking her back, i.e., jiggling the child gently. 旨く泣き已む事もある sometimes he nicely (i.e., to her convenience) stops crying. 又 on the other hand. 泣き立てる to cry hard in a loud voice. いずれにしても whichever is the case. 容易に立たない [the mother] does not easily rise [from her crouched prayer position].

8. 一通り夫の身の上を祈ってしまうと when she finishes one round of praying for her husband's safety. 細帯を解いて……脊中から前へ廻して she loosens the thin sash [used to carry the child on her back], and as if to slide him down, brings him from her back to front [to hold him in both arms]. 拝殿を上がって行って i.e., 拝殿の階段を上がっていって. 待って御出よ wait here for me; short for 待っておいでなさいよ. きっと (- - -) with a swift or tense motion; (- - -) without fail. その片端を拝殿の欄干に括り付ける ties the other end [of the narrow sash] to the railing of the worship hall. 段々 steps, 階段. 二十間の敷石を往ったり来たり back and forth along 20 *ken* of paving stones. 御百度を踏む (- - - - - - -) to walk back and forth one hundred times between a certain spot in the shrine or temple complex and the worship place, repeating a prayer each time.

9. 細帯の丈のゆるす限り (the child crawled about) as widely as the length of the narrow sash [that tied the child to the railing] allowed. 広縁 the broad verandah [of the worship hall]. 〜に取(と)って for [the mother]; now always written with hiragana only. 甚だ楽な夜 quite an easy night. ひいひい泣かれると when [the child tied to the railing] cries and cries. 気が気ではない to feel extremely uneasy; anxious. すかして置いて after coaxing / cajoling [the child]. 踏み直す to resume [the *ohyakudo* prayers].

10. 幾晩となく countless evenings; night after night. 気を揉んで worrying. 夜の目も寝ずに without getting a wink of sleep all night. とくの昔に long before; とうの昔に、とっくの昔に. 浪士 masterless samurai.

る。又益々烈しく泣き立てる事もある。いずれにしても母は容易に立たない。

（八）一通り夫の身の上を祈って仕舞うと、今度は細帯を解いて、脊中の子を摺り卸ろすように、脊中から前へ廻して、両手に抱きながら拝殿を上って行って、「好い子だから、少しの間、待って御出よ」と屹度自分の頬を子供の頬へ擦り附ける。そうして細帯を長くして、子供を縛って置いて、その片端を拝殿の欄干に括り附ける。それから段々を下りて来て二十間の敷石を往ったり来たり御百度を踏む。

（九）拝殿に括りつけられた子は、暗闇の中で、細帯の丈のゆるす限り、広縁の上を這い廻っている。そういう時は母に取って、甚だ楽な夜である。けれども縛った子にひいひい泣かれると、母は気が気でない。御百度の足が非常に早くなる。大変息が切れる。仕方のない時は、中途で拝殿へ上って来て、色々すかして置いて、又御百度を踏す事もある。

一〇　こう云う風に、幾晩となく母が気を揉んで、夜の目も寝ずに心配していた父は、とくの昔に浪士の為に殺されていたのである。

こんな悲しい話を、夢の中で母から聞いた。

第十夜

1. 庄太郎 The same character appeared in the Eighth Night, in a panama hat and accompanied by a woman. Aside from the early Kamakura sculptor Unkei in the Sixth Night, Shōtarō and Ken-san in this dream are the only characters with proper names. 女に攫われてから since having been kidnapped by a woman. ふらりと (mimesis) without advance notice; without any particular purpose, accidentally. どっと、床に就いている has suddenly taken to bed.

2. 町内一の好男子 best looking man in town. 至極善良な正直者 extremely good-natured and honest person. 道楽 hobby, enjoyment, pastime. パナマの帽子 panama hat; see 第八夜. 夕方 Depending upon the edition, the pronunciation choice is ゆうがた, which is more common. 水菓子屋 fruit shop, now 果物屋 (くだものや). 店先へ腰をかけて seated in front of the store. Benches were often put out before stores. 往来 street; traffic. これと云う程の特色 any particular characteristic / idiosyncrasy worth mentioning.

3. 水蜜桃 juicy peach developed from a Shanghai variety. Most peaches are still of this kind today. 枇杷 loquat. 奇麗に籠に盛る to arrange [fruit] neatly in a basket. すぐ見舞物（土産物）に持って行ける様に so that they can be taken as gifts right away [without having to gift-wrap them]. 二列に [baskets of the fruit stand] in two rows. 庄太郎はこの籠を見ては Shōtarō looks again and again at these baskets [and with each look comments that they are pretty]. は indicates repetition. 商売をするなら水菓子屋に限る if you do business, a fruit shop is the only way to go. その癖 自分はパナマの帽子を被ってぶらぶら遊んでいる for all that, he himself is idling away the time in his panama hat.

4. この色がいゝ (- - , - - - - - with stress on ろ rather than - - - - - - -) the color is what distinguishes this fruit (rather than "this color is good"). 夏蜜柑 sour, thick-rinded, larger summer citrus not quite as large as grapefruit. を品評する to appraise. 曾て銭を出して水菓子を買った事がない never paid money to buy fruit. 只では無論食わない of course he eats none for free; if he doesn't pay of course he does not eat any.

5. 不意に suddenly; with no advance notice. 身分のある人と見えて seemingly a person of some social status. 立派な服装をしている she was finely dressed. 大事なパナマの帽子を脱って taking off his precious panama hat and greeted her politely.

第十夜

一　庄太郎が女に攫われてから七日目の晩にふらりと帰って来て、急に熱が出てどっと、床に就いていると云って健さんが知らせに来た。

二　庄太郎は町内一の好男子で、至極善良な正直者である。ただ一つの道楽がある。パナマの帽子を被って、夕方になると水菓子屋の店先へ腰をかけて、往来の女の顔を眺めている。そうして頻に感心している。其の外には是と云う程の特色もない。

三　あまり女が通らない時は、往来を見ないで水菓子を見ている。水菓子には色々ある。水蜜桃や林檎や、枇杷や、バナヽを奇麗に籠に盛って、すぐ見舞物に持って行ける様に二列に並べてある。庄太郎は此の籠を見ては奇麗だと云っている。商売をするなら水菓子屋に限ると云っている。其の癖自分はパナマの帽子を被ってぶらヽ遊んでいる。

四　此の色がいヽと云って、夏蜜柑抔を品評する事もある。けれども、曾て銭を出して水菓子を買った事がない。只では無論食わない。色許り賞めて居る。

五　ある夕方一人の女が、不意に店先に立った。身分のある人と見えて立派な服装をしている。其の着物の色がひどく庄太郎の気に入った。其の上庄太郎は大変女の顔に感心して仕舞った。そこで大事な

籠詰 a basket of fruit.　　云うんで (*colloq.*) 云うので.　　それを一寸提げて見て holding [the basket] in her hand for a second [to see if she could manage it].　　大変重い事 (*female expression*) how very heavy.

6. 元来閑人の上に on top of being a man of leisure from the beginning.　　頗る気作な extremely easy-going / willing / open-hearted.　　ではお宅迄持って参りましょう then let me carry it to your home.　　それぎり（それきり）帰って来なかった he never returned; that was the last sight of him.

7. 如何な (from 如何なる) 庄太郎でも whatever Shōtarō's nature is / even with Shōtarō's relaxed nature.　　余り呑気過ぎる this is too carefree.　　只事じゃ無かろう perhaps it's no ordinary event; it may be serious; ただごとではないだろう.　騒ぎ出していると when [relatives and friends] began loudly expressing their worries.　寄ってたかって crowding together around him.

8. 何でも余程長い電車に違いない details aside, it must have been quite a long train ride.　　原 grassy field.　　何処を見廻しても whichever direction one looked; as far as one's eyes could see.　　絶壁の天辺 the top of a cliff. 絶壁（ぜっぺき）is *ateji* for 切岸. The pronunciation preference is きりぎし depending upon the edition. 此処から飛び込んで御覧なさい try plunging in from here; see if you can jump. 底を覗いて見ると when he peered at the bottom.　　再三辞退した repeatedly declined.　　もし思い切って飛び込まなければ if you don't make up your mind and jump.　　豚に舐められますが好う御座んすか you'll be licked by the pigs; is that all right? 舐める, "to lick," also means "to make light of." 好う御座んすか is polite but less formal than ようございますか.　　雲右衛門 Tōchūken Kumoemon (桃中軒雲右衛門, 1873-1916), or his brand of Naniwabushi. Kumoemon, né Okamoto Minekichi, a master Naniwabushi narrator at age 13, later developed a narrative style in praise of the way of samurai, and succeeded in bringing Naniwabushi, till then a street form of music, into the theater. In 1907, the year before *Yume jūya* was written, Kumoemon performed at the Hongōza in Tokyo before a full house on 27 successive days.　　命には易えられない nothing can replace life; life is the most important thing.　　飛び込むのを見合わせていた he was putting off jumping.　　ところへ thereupon; right then.　　鼻を鳴らして grunting.　　檳榔樹の洋杖 rattan walking stick. This recalls the magic wand with which Circe changed Ulysses' companions into pigs and back into men again.　　鼻頭 muzzle; snout.　　ぐうと云いながら with a stifled noise in its throat. ぐう is a choking sound let out in response to a fall or an attack.　　ころりと引っ繰り返って somersaulting. ころりと (*mimesis*) applies to an easy, effortless, sudden motion or action (often of a round thing).

パナマの帽子を脱って丁寧に挨拶をしたら、女は籠詰の一番大きいのを指して、是を下さいと云うんで、庄太郎はすぐに其の籠を取って渡した。すると女はそれを一寸提げて見て、大変重い事だと云った。

庄太郎は元来閑人の上に、頗る気作な男だから、ではお宅迄持って参りましょうと云って、女と一所に水菓子屋を出た。それぎり帰って来なかった。

如何な庄太郎でも、余まり呑気過ぎる。只事じゃ無かろうと云って、親類や友達が騒ぎ出して居る所に、七日目の晩になって、ふらりと帰って来た。そこで大勢寄ってたかって、庄さん何処へ行っていたんだいと聞くと、庄太郎は電車へ乗って山へ行ったんだと答えた。

何でも余程長い電車に違いない。庄太郎の云う所によると、電車を下りるとすぐと原へ出たそうである。非常に広い原で、何処を見廻しても青い草ばかり生えていた。女と一所に草の上を歩いて行くと、急に絶壁の天辺へ出た、其の時女が庄太郎に、此処から飛び込んで御覧なさいと云った。底を覗いて見ると、切岸は見えるが底は見えない。庄太郎は又パナマの帽子を脱いで再三辞退した。すると女が、もし思い切って飛び込まなければ、豚に舐められますが好う御座んすかと聞いた。庄太郎は豚と雲右衛門が大嫌いだった。けれども命には易えられないと思って、矢っ張り飛び込むのを見合わせていた。所へ豚が一匹鼻を鳴らして来た。庄太郎は仕方なしに、持って居た細い檳榔樹の洋杖で、豚の鼻頭を打った。豚はぐうと云いながら、ころりと引っ繰り返って、絶壁の下へ落ちて行った。庄太

ほっと一と息接いでいると as he was giving a sigh of relief.　　大きな鼻を庄太郎に擦り附けに来た [another pig] came to rub his large snout against Shōtarō.　　已を得ず unavoidably; out of necessity.　　真逆様に headlong.　　遥の青草原の尽きる辺から from where the far-reaching field of green grass ended; from beyond the far-reaching grassy field.　　幾万匹か数え切れぬ豚 countless pigs, perhaps tens of thousands.　　群をなして in a big crowd. The usual reading of 群 in this phrase is むれ, which is the pronunciation choice depending upon the edition; also written 群れをなして. *It has been pointed out that this imagery recalls the large herd of swine that was feeding at a distance but, as two demons (or an unclean spirit) entered it, rushed down the steep bank into the water and perished (Matthew, 8: 28-34; Mark, 5: 1-13; Luke, 8: 26-33), and that while in London Sōseki may have seen Briton Riviere's oil painting, "The Miracle of the Gadarene Swine," 1883, Tate Gallery (Iwanami's Sōseki zenshū, 1994, vol. 12, p. 658).*　　を見懸けて（目掛けて）making for / heading for.　心から恐縮した [Shōtarō] was thoroughly frightened / impressed.　　洋杖が鼻へ触りさえすれば all that was necessary was for the stick to touch a pig's muzzle [requiring no hitting]; at the lightest touch of the stick on a pig's snout.　　行列して in file; in procession.　　我ながら despite himself.　　続々 one after another.　　黒雲に足が生えて、青草を踏み分ける様な勢いで forcefully as if a dark cloud had formed legs and was striding over the green grass.　　無尽蔵に with an inexhaustible supply; endlessly.

9. 必死の勇を振って mustering desperate courage.　　精根が尽きて、手が蒟蒻の様に弱って his energy exhausted, his arm weak [and trembling] like taro-root jelly.　仕舞に in the end [he was licked by the pigs].

10. 自分も尤もだと思った I too thought [what Ken said] reasonable / convincing. *The fake innocence produces humor.*　　助かるまい will not probably survive.

郎はほっと一と息接いでいると又一匹の豚が大きな鼻を庄太郎に擦り附けに来た。庄太郎は已を得ず又洋杖を振り上げた。豚はぐうと鳴いて又真逆様に穴の底へ転げ込んだ。すると又一匹あらわれた。

此の時庄太郎は不図気が附いて、向うを見ると、遥の青草原の尽きる辺りから幾万匹か数え切れぬ豚が、群をなして一直線に、此の絶壁の上に立っている庄太郎を見懸けて鼻を鳴らしてくる。庄太郎は心から恐縮した。けれども仕方がないから、近寄ってくる豚の鼻頭を、一つ一つ丁寧に檳榔樹の洋杖で打っていた。不思議な事に洋杖が鼻へ触りさえすれば豚はころりと谷の底へ落ちて行く。覗いて見ると底の見えない絶壁を、逆さになった豚が行列して落ちて行く。自分が此の位多くの豚を谷へ落したかと思うと、庄太郎は我ながら怖くなった。けれども豚は続々くる。黒雲に足が生えて、青草を踏み分ける様な勢いで無尽蔵に鼻を鳴らしてくる。

庄太郎は必死の勇を振って、豚の鼻頭を七日六晩叩いた。けれども、とうとう精根が尽きて、手が蒟蒻の様に弱って、仕舞に豚に舐められてしまった。そうして絶壁の上へ倒れた。

健さんは、庄太郎の話を此処迄して、だから余り女を見るのは善くないよと云った。自分も尤もだと思った。けれども健さんは庄太郎のパナマの帽子が貰いたいと云っていた。

庄太郎は助かるまい。パナマは健さんのものだろう。

明治四一、七、二五―八、五

坂の上の闇

富岡多恵子

Darkness Atop the Slope

Tomioka Taeko

TOMIOKA TAEKO was born in 1935 into a scrap iron dealer's family in a working class Ōsaka neighborhood. While attending Ōsaka National Women's University as an English major, in 1957 she privately published her first anthology, *Henrei* (Courtesy in Return; tr. *See You Soon*), for which she received the H poetry prize. On graduating, she taught high school briefly before moving to Tōkyō in 1960. She largely stopped writing poetry soon after her 1965-66 visit to the United States during which she lived in downtown Manhattan for several months. Her complete poems were published in 1967. Tomioka's first fictional work, "Facing the Hills They Stand," appeared in 1971. With this novella about two generations of a family that settled by an Ōsaka river, she distinguished herself as a superb storyteller. Since then Tomioka has published numerous works of fiction, as well as movie and radio scripts, plays, essays, an autobiography, a recorded album of original songs, and critical works.

Tomioka's full-length novels include *Shokubutsusai* (1973, Ritual of Plants), *Kochūan ibun* (1974, Strange Accounts of Kochūan), *Namiutsu tochi* (1983, Undulating Land), *Byakkō* (1988, White Light), *Sakagami* (1990), and *Hiberunia-tō kikō* (1997, A Journey to Ireland). She received the Noma Literary Prize for *Hiberunia-tō kikō*, a travelogue that is at once a study of Jonathan Swift and an inquiry into the modes of life and death.

Among her collections of short stories and novellas are *Oka ni mukatte hito wa narabu* (1976, tr. "Facing the Hills They Stand"), *Dōbutsu no sōrei* (1975; tr. *The Funeral of a Giraffe*), *Tōsei bonjin den* (1977, Lives of Common People Today), *Han'myō* (1979, Blister Beetle), *Sūku* (1980, Straw Dogs), and *Tōi sora* (1982, Distant Sky). *Meido no kazoku* (1974, A Family of the Underworld) is a semi-autobiographical tetralogy. *Tomioka Taeko no Kōshoku Gonin Onna* (1986, Tomioka Taeko's Five Women Who Loved Love) is a modern Japanese translation of Saikaku's *Kōshoku gonin on'na* (1686, tr. *Five Women Who Loved Love*, 1956) and *Kōshoku ichidai on'na* (1686, tr. *Life of an Amorous Woman*, 1963). This and *Chikamatsu jōruri shikō* (1978, Personal Views of Chikamatsu's Puppet Plays) typically reflect her profound understanding of the traditional Kansai narrative-theatrical arts that were familiar to her from early on. Her interest in Saikaku led to writing another book called *Saikakuno kanjō* (2004, Saikaku's Sentiment), which examines the *ukiyozōshi* prose (stories mostly about townspeople and deep human feelings) of one who was also a *haikai* poet. *Naka Kansuke no koi* (1994, Naka Kansuke in Love) explores the psychology of the novelist and poet Naka Kansuke. *Shaku Chōkū nōto* (2000, Notes on Shaku Chōkū), winner of the Mainichi shuppan bunkashō (Mainichi cultural award on outstanding publications), is a study of the tanka of Shaku Chōkū (1887-1953, real name Orikuchi Shinobu), Ōsaka-born poet and scholar of Japanese literature and folklore. *Naniwa tomo are koto no yoshiashi* (Naniwa or Whatever, Reed or Rush for Good or Bad, 2005), is a collection of essays, many on Ōsaka and its dialect. Although spending major portions of her adult years in Tokyo, she very much remains in spirit a Kansai intellectual. Tomioka also co-authored, with Ueno Chizuko and Ogura Chikako, *Danryū bungakuron* (1989, On the Male School of Literature), a hard-hitting feminist critique of well-known Japanese male authors.

"Saka no ue no yami" (Darkness Atop the Slope) is the first of five novellas collected in *Sūku*. The story begins with an inscrutable late eighteenth century event that occurred at a pleasure house near the Ise Shrine.

WORKS IN ENGLISH TRANSLATION

See You Soon (Henrei). Hiroaki Sato, tr. Chicago Review Press, 1979. ("See You Soon" and "Courtesy in Return" (henrei) are both titles of poems appearing in the volume.)

"Facing the Hills They Stand" (Oka ni mukatte hito wa narabu). Kyoko Selden, tr., in *Japanese Women Writers: Twentieth Century Short Fiction* (M. E. Sharpe, 1982, revised 1991), Mizuta Noriko Lippit and Kyoko Iriye Selden, eds. and trs.

"Straw Dogs" (Sūku). In *Unmapped Territories: New Women's Fiction* (Women in Translation, 1991), Yukiko Tanaka, tr.

The Funeral of a Giraffe: Seven Stories by Tomioka Taeko (Dōbutsu no sōrei). Kyoko Selden and Mizuta Noriko, trs. M. E. Sharpe, 2000.

1. 伊勢古市の、間の山と呼ばれる尾部坂をのぼりきった長峯丘陵の最高所 に at the highest point of the Nagamine Hills, in Furuichi in Ise province, at the end of a climb along the Obe Slope, known as "Ai no Yama" (the Slope Between). 伊勢古市, Furuichi in Ise province (now Mie prefecture), is located in present day Ise city in the western part of Mie prefecture. Located along the old highway between the Inner and Outer Shrines (see 50), inns and pleasure houses prospered in the Edo period with the growing popularity of visits to the Shrine. 間の山 was a popular name for 長峰丘陵, a hilly area along the old highway between the the Inner and Outer Shrines. The name now refers to 尾部坂. 妓楼油屋 a pleasure house by the name of Aburaya. The name suggests that it was formerly an oil dealer. 敷地三千坪とかいわれた広大な土地 a spacious lot that was rumored to be 3,000 *tsubo* wide (approximately 12,000 square yards). 〜に割って入るように as if to edge in, obtrude, or interfere. *The subject is the train tracks.*

2. 〜なる男 a man by the name of 〜. なる, the noun modifier form of なり (an auxiliary verb of affirmation, similar to *mod. J.* である). 寛政八年 1796. 寛政 is the name of an Edo period era that lasted from 1789 to 1800. 節句 seasonal festival. Here it refers to the May 5th festival that celebrates the health and growth of boys. 宵宮 also called *yoimatsuri* (宵祭り) is a small festival held the night before. 長峯二十余町 over twenty *chō* of the Nagamine slope; one *chō* is approximately 119 yards. 軒をつらね standing side by side. 軒 means eaves of a house. 古市遊廓最盛期 the peak period of the pleasure quarters of Furuichi. 年のころ、二十七、八歳 twenty-seven or eight years of age. 年のころ is a fixed phrase and is prefixed directly before someone's age. 総髪 "total hair"; hair combed back, tied or not tied in back, as opposed to the Edo top-knot style with the front part of the head shaven. Those who wore this hairstyle included doctors, Confucian scholars, Shintō officials, *yamabushi* (mountain ascetics), and *rōnin* (masterless samurai). 色白の美男子 fair- complexioned, good-looking (young) man.

3. 中居 a maid at brothels and restaurants who hosts guests with food and drinks. The term also meant a rear chamber for maids in the Shogunate palace or a daimyō mansion, or maids who served there; a lowest-rank monk in a temple; or a middle-rank maid in an Edo period merchant household. 万乃 a female name pronounced Mano as a Man'yō-gana name (in which each kanji represents Japanese syllables phonetically). The head maid's name in real life was お万 (Oman with a prefix "o" common to female names in premodern times). In the kabuki play mentioned below, it is Mano (written 万野). 商売柄 as her occupation required. とりとめないこと rambling, unfocused chat; small talk. 愛想よく amiably; agreeably. さえずり (囀り) twittering, chattering. 伊勢音頭にまじって

坂の上の闇

一

伊勢古市の、間の山と呼ばれる尾部坂をのぼりきった長峯丘陵の最高所に、妓楼油屋があった。敷地三千坪とかいわれた広大な土地に割って入るように、現在は電車が走っている。寛政八年の五月四日のことである。その夜

二

夜の十一時ごろ、福間一紀なる男が油屋の客となった。当時は妓楼が七十軒くらい軒をつらね、古市遊廓最盛期であった。油屋に入ってきた男は、年のころ、二十七、八歳の総髪で、色白の美男子であった。男は、ひとりで油屋に入ってきた。

三

男を仲居の万乃が部屋へ案内した。万乃は商売柄、とりとめないことを愛想よく喋りつづけていた。

mingled with an Ise song. Ise-ondo is a collective name for folk songs that originated in Edo era in Ise and spread throughout the country as visits to the Ise Shrine became popular. In particular, it refers to a nagauta-style dance song composed in the Kyōhō era (1716-1735), which was popular at Furuichi and other pleasure quarters. It is also short for *Ise-ondo koi no netaba* (伊勢音頭恋寝刃), a kabuki play based on the Aburaya incident narrated here. See 85.　　おこん　the name of a geisha. Women's names were often written in hiragana prior to modern times. Cf. き さ, the name of the mother of Aburaya's proprietor Seiemon; よし、きし and しか, the names of other Aburaya female employees mentioned in later paragraphs.　　敵 娼におこんをあてがった　assigned Okon [to Ikki] as a partner for the evening. 敵娼 means a courtesan or a young man who waits upon a guest at a pleasure house. Written 相方 or 合方, the term also means musical accompaniment.　　客あしら いにもの慣れた、その場限りの軽々しいもの　manners suggestive of being used to handling customers and put on for the occasion.　　他人に喋っている様子を聞 くと　when hearing the way [Mano] spoke to others.

4. この伊勢の者か　Are you from Ise right here?　　敵娼に身の上を聞く野暮 に　[Ikki paid no attention] to his inelegance in asking his partner her personal background. *Yabo* (野暮), the inexperienced, is opposed to *tsū* (通), the experienced, who knew how to treat courtesans in their roles and refrain from asking personal questions, partly from an understanding that many were bought from poor, rural families. The inexperienced tended to lack playfulness and would attempt to converse on a personal level.　　一日に五千人といわれた　[Ise-visitors] who were said to number 5,000 per day.　　宇治　a place name in southern Kyōto prefecture on the Uji river. The area is known for the eleventh century temple Byōdōin, as the setting of the final ten chapters of the *Tale of Genji,* and for fine tea called Ujicha. 伊勢参りのヨソ者、旅人客でないこと　[Ikki wished to let Okon know] that he was one of the strangers visiting the Ise Shrine, in other words, a travelling customer. 陰気な客の気分を逆転させる手管　the knack of reversing the customer's dark mood.　　田舎くさい様子で　looking rustic.　　どこの在所の娘かと思わせ、く にをたずねさせたのだった　[Okon's looks] had made [Ikki] wonder which village she was from and ask where her native place was. *The use of hiragana for* く に *and* たずねる *here is characteristic of Tomioka's writing. Hiragana, often in an expressive and esthetically appealing way, restores Japanese words to their sounds by dissociating them from kanji meanings (here* 国、邦；尋ねる、訊ねる、 訪ねる). 二の腕が出てきた　a [fat, tanned] forearm showed. 二の腕 means either the upper or lower arm. Instead of pouring rice wine with both hands, a courtesan pours with her right hand while holding her sleeve back from underneath with her left hand.　　開業する　to practice [medicine], start [a store].　　さすがにそこ

万乃のさえずりは、あちこちから聞こえてくる伊勢音頭にまじって、一紀にはよく耳に入らなかった。敵娼におこんをあてがったのは万乃であった。年は十五だといった。一紀は黙って酒を飲みつづけた。おこんも黙っていた。時折、万乃が客を案内する声が部屋の外で聞えた。その喋り方、声の出し方、笑い方は、いかにも客あしらいにもの慣れた、その場限りの軽々しいものに思えた。他人に喋っている様子を聞くと、一紀にはこと

部屋に入ってしばらくひとりで酒を飲んでいると、おこんがきた。

さらにそれがよく感じられた。

四

この伊勢の者かと一紀はおこんにたずねた。おこんは黙っていた。敵娼に身の上をきく野暮に、一紀は無頓着であった。自分は宇治の者だと一紀はいった。陰気に酒を飲んだ。一紀は、そのころ一日に五千人といわれた伊勢まいりのヨソ者、旅人客でないことをいいたかった。おこんには、陰気な客の気分を逆転させる手管がまだなかった。ただ田舎くさい様子で坐っていた。その様子が、一紀に、どこの在所の娘かと思わせ、くにをたずねさせたのだった。酒をつぐのに伸ばすおこんの手が一紀の目に入った。京都ではこういう田舎くさい女を見たことはなかった。おこんが知るはずはなかった。自分は京都にいたんだ、と一紀はいった。おこんはあまり驚かなかった。一紀は、三年間の京都留学ののち、一年ほど前から宇治浦田町に於て開業している医者であった。しかし、さすがにそこまでは女に喋らなかった。ただ、

この在所の娘かと思わせ、くにをたずねさせたのだった。京都を知っているかと一紀はいった。ふとい、色のくろい二の腕が出てきた。

までは女に喋らなかった [Ikki] did not, inexperienced as he was, tell her that much.　　つるつるすべるような声をあげて raising a voice that sounded slippery smooth. つるつる *(mimesis)* describes a glossy, slippery, difficult to grasp condition. *The smooth tone here conveys the insincerely pleasant, elusive manners of a woman experienced in handling customers.*　　ふすま越しに from behind a sliding door.

5. つい先ほど二階に三四人であがっていったらしい客の声 the voices of the three or four customers who seemed to have gone up to the second floor just a while ago.　　手にとるように as vividly as if taking [the sound, image, etc.] in hand. どうやら油屋の上客らしく apparently favored patrons of Aburaya.　　その席にいる女達の声も数人らしく聞きとれる from the sound of it, there seemed to be several geisha in their room.　　ふいに爆発のように響き [men's laughter] suddenly rang like an explosion.　　野太い robust.　　役者の声色 mimicry of a stage actor's speech.　　芝居小屋 theater.　　その帰りかも知れない [the men] might have stopped by here on their way home from the theater.　　一紀のような地元の客があがる方がめずらしい it was rarer for a local customer like Ikki to visit. あがる here is synonymous with 登楼する (to visit a geisha house).　　伊勢参りの精進落としの場所 a place for ending the religious abstinence required when visiting the Ise Shrine.　　陽気に、派手に 遊んで、金を落とす客 customers who squandered their money on raucous fun.

6. 想像がつく it is easy to imagine.　　その二階の客のにぎわいがもはやおさまっても even when the merriment of the patrons on the second floor had already subsided.　　といって though that being the case; and yet.　　どうしてもおこんでなければならぬとせつに思って酒を飲んでいるわけではなかった it was not that [Ikki] was drinking here expressly for the pleasure of Okon's company.

おこんが、京都にいたという一紀に、どうして京都に、とたずねたら答えたかもしれなかった。その時、つるつるすべるような声をあげて、万乃がふすま越しに、おこんをちょっとの間借りますといって呼びにきた。一紀はひとりになった。

五　ひとりで酒を飲んでいると、一紀にはまわりの音や声が急によく聞こえて思えた。とりわけ、つい先ほど二階に三、四人であがっていったらしい客の声が手にとるように一紀には聞える。どうやら油屋の上客らしく、その席にいる女たちの声も数人らしく聞きとれる。

ちの笑い声がふいに爆発のように響き、女たちの笑い声もそれを追いかけている。笑い声にまじって喋る男の野太い声も聞える。役者の声色らしいのも聞える。長峯には芝居小屋がある。その帰りかもしれない。しかしその喋る言葉の調子はこの土地の者ではない。伊勢まいりの帰りの地方の客か、一年に一度ここにくる商人だろう。油屋には、一紀のような地元の客があがる方がめずらしい。古市間の山は、伊勢まいりの精進落しの場所である。ひとりで陰気に酒を飲む客などこの夜も一紀の他にはいない。陽気に、派手に遊んで、金を落す客がこういう場所の上客だ。

六　かなりの間、一紀はひとりで酒を飲んでいたが、おこんは戻ってこなかった。二階で派手にやっている客の方へまわっているらしいことは想像がつく。ところが、その二階の客のにぎわいがもはやおさまってもおこんは戻らない。といって、一紀は、どうしてもおこんでなければならぬとせつに思っ

女がおればいいのである as long as there was a woman [to serve his drinks] he didn't mind.　一紀とて、妓楼のまわしという 商法を知らぬわけではない even Ikki was not ignorant of the pleasure-house business practice of a courtesan serving more than one customer. まわし literally means "passing around," thus referring also to a cape, a sumō wrestler's belt, appropriating money for a different purpose, and negotiating schedules.　下女 maidservant.　酒を運んできていた had brought sake.　その酒がきれたところで just as the sake ran out.

7. 目ざとく（目敏く）見つけ detecting quickly.　ひきとめるやら、謝るやら now persuading him to stay and now apologizing.　かしましく（姦しく）言葉を一紀にあびせた（浴びせた）loudly, noisily showered Ikki with words.　その言葉に反応せぬ一紀に向かって to Ikki who did not respond to those words.　いかにも野暮天と言わぬばかりに looking precisely as if to say Ikki was a boor. 陽気にまくしたててきた cheerfully rattled on at him. まくしたてる (lit.) to talk fast rolling the tongue.　待ちくたぶれて [a man on his way home] having tired of waiting [for a woman]. くたぶれる is a colloquial form of くたびれる. ちょっとからかうような、またなぐさめる ような、一種の親愛のごとき色あい an air of affection of a sort, slightly teasing and also consolatory.　女郎を采配する中居頭らしいしっかり者 a responsible person, as befitting a head maid (that she is) who manages prostitutes.　いかにもこういう商売の水を飲んできた女の、薄情そうな風情と、ひとなつっこさ（人懐っこさ）a cold-hearted air and a social ease, very much of a woman who has drunk the water of this kind of trade. ひとなつっこさ is from ひとなつこい amiable, friendly, quick to take kindly to people (as with a domestic animal).　裏腹に back to back.　そのやせぎすの身のこなしにあらわれていた [the opposite qualities] showed in the way Mano carried her slender body. 身のこなし, deportment.　子供に念をおしてものを渡すよう as if handing an object to a child with careful instruction. 念をおす（押す）means to emphasize or underscore.　心もち口をまげ、笑みをこらえ、あごを引き、首を傾げて just slightly curling her lips, restraining a smile, with chin drawn in and head inclined to one side.　その、万乃の様子に反応するように as if to respond to this gesture of Mano.　刀の鞘を左手でつかんだ grasped the sword by the hilt with his left hand. ふいに（不意に）unpremeditatedly, unthinkingly, suddenly.

て酒を飲んでいるわけではなかった。今ここにだれか酒の相手に女がおればいいのである。一紀とて、妓楼のまわしという商法を知らぬわけではない。

おこんが部屋から出ていって一紀はひとりでいた。その間に、下女が二度酒を運んできていた。ちょうど、その酒がきれたところで、一紀は立ち上った。

部屋を出てきた一紀を、万乃が目ざとく見つけ、ひきとめるやら、謝るやら、かしましく言葉を一紀にあびせた。その言葉に反応せぬ一紀に向って、今度はいかにも野暮天といわぬばかりに万乃は陽気にまくしたててきた。一紀は、きた時にあずけた刀を万乃から受けとった。刀を渡す時、万乃は、小さい目を見開いて、一紀をにらむように見た。その目付きには、女を待ちくたぶれて帰る男をちょっとからかうような、またなぐさめるような、一種の親愛のごとき色あいも見えたが、一紀にはそれが感じとれなかった。万乃は、女郎を采配する仲居頭らしいしっかり者で、いかにもこういう商売の水を飲んできた女の、薄情そうな風情と、ひとなつっこさが、裏腹にその痩せぎすの身のこなしにあらわれていた。刀を、一紀の掌に、子供に念を押してものを渡すよう万乃は押しつけた。そして、心もち口をまげ笑みをこらえ、顎を引き、首をかしげて一紀を見た。その、万乃の様子に反応するように、一紀も真面目な顔付きで刀の鞘を左手でつかんだ。そしてふいに、右手でものものしく刀を半分抜き、万乃の方を見た。万乃は、子供のいたずらを見た時のように、わざと目を見はり口を開けて驚いた様

半分引き抜いた刀を、すうっと先の方まで抜いていった continued to draw the already half-drawn sword smoothly all the way out of the sheath to the tip of the blade.　　刀をこうして引き抜くなんてことは、一紀には今までなかった drawing his sword like this had never until then happened to Ikki. なんてことは is colloquial for なんていうことは.　　引き抜いた刀をだらりと床に向けて holding the drawn sword loosely with its tip pointing at the floor. だらりと (*onomat.*) describes a loose, unfocused, dangling manner.　　機嫌をとるように as if to humor [Ikki].

8. 刀を振り上げ、万乃の横で刀をかまえて見せた swung his sword with both hands above his head, then held it at the ready by Mano's side as a gesture, i.e., for her to see, or to see how she would react.　　ふざけて万乃を 威嚇しているように見えた [Ikki] seemed to threaten Mano in jest.　　アレアレ、マア oh my, oh my.　　子供をはやしたて、またいたずらを とどめるような声をあげた [Mano] raised a voice that was like cheering on a child, and also like restraining a child from a naughty prank.　　かまえた刀をもう一度振りあげ、振りおろした [Ikki] swung the sword he had held at the ready once again above his head, then brought it down.　　異様に高い声をはりあげ（張り上げ） raising an abnormally high-pitched voice; in an unusually loud voice.　　指三本を斬った cut off three fingers. The kanji 斬 is often preferred to 切 for slaying with a sword.　　奥の方 へかけこんで（駆け込んで）いった [Mano] ran toward the back rooms.　　その、 人殺しという声に誘われるように as though drawn in by that voice that cried "murder!"

9. 下男 man servant.　　はらいのける（払い除ける）ようにして as if to brush [Ukichi] away.　　下女のよし the maidservant Yoshi.　　出合頭に on coming out.

子をした。一紀も、万乃に、いたずらをわざと見せるような様子であった。一紀は万乃の顔を見ながら、半分引き抜いた刀を、すうっと先の方まで抜いていった。刀をこうして引き抜くなんてことは、一紀に今までなかった。引き抜いた刀をだらりと床に向けて、一紀はもう一度万乃の顔を見た。万乃は、不思議なものを見るように刀を見、それから一紀の顔を見上げて、機嫌をとるようにかすかに笑った。

ハ　その時、一紀はふいに刀を振り上げ、万乃の横で刀をかまえて見せた。それは子供がおもちゃの刀をかまえて見せているようだった。一紀はふざけて万乃を威嚇しているように見えた。万乃はアレアレ、マァ、と子供をはやしたて、またいたずらをとどめるような声をあげた。一紀はかまえた刀をもう一度振りあげ、振りおろした。それが、アレアレ、といいながら手をあげて、一紀の遊びをとめようとしている万乃の手に触れ、指三本を斬った。万乃は、助けて！りあげ、奥の方へかけこんでいった。人殺し！　人殺し！　という万乃の声が何度も何度も響いた。

その、人殺しという声に誘われるように、一紀は奥へ入っていった。

九　万乃の声に驚いて下男の卯吉が奥からかけ出してきた。その卯吉を一紀ははらいのけるようにして、腕を斬った。次に下女のよしが出てきたが、出合頭に左の肩先と左手指を斬られて倒れた。家の中が揺れるようにざわめきはじめた。一紀は、さらに奥へ踏みこんでいき、油屋の家族のいる部屋のふす

ふすま（襖）sliding door.　　おびえて（怯えて）frightened.　　きさの頭めがけて斬りおろした swung his sword down, aiming at Kisa's head.　　肩をかすめた（掠めた）[his sword] brushed her shoulder.　　えぐるように（抉るように）斬った cut with a gouging motion.　　それで [died] from that blow.

10.　血にまみれた blood-smeared.　　ころげる（転げる）ように almost tumbling down.　　待ちぶせるようにして as though ambushing [Kishi].　　思い切り with all his might, with determination.　　首は半分落ちかかるくらいに斬られ、きしは即死した her head was cut so deeply that it nearly hung loose halfway and Kishi died instantly.　　重なるように [three men came down the stairs] as if tumbling over one another. *These men are patrons; not male servants, who work downstairs.*　　いずれも重傷を負うて倒れた all three fell, each suffering a serious wound. 負うて, obsolete in standard dialect, is another form of 負って. Other examples of a connective + て, where うて occurs instead of the expected って: 言う→言うて instead of 言って in Kansai; 問う→問うて in standard dialect as well.

11.　倒れた人間を足で払いのけるようにして as if kicking the fallen people out of the way with his feet. *The use of the word 人間 is strikingly objective, pointing to the fact that those slain were objects to Ikki, as becomes clearer in the following passages.*　　一瞬のうちに人が斬られる様 appearance/sight/way in which people were slain in a flash.　　部屋から飛び出してきた者はどこかに逃げたのだった those who had dashed out of the rooms had fled somewhere. This clause ends with のだった (the fact is that. . .) because it clarifies the reason that Ikki found no one when he came out to the front.

まを蹴った。そこには、油屋主人清右衛門の母親きさがおびえて坐っていた。一紀はきさの頭めがけて斬りおろしたが、きさが転倒したので肩をかすめた。さらにもう一度肩から腕を斬り、倒れたきさを踏みつけて、乳の下をえぐるように斬った。きさはそれで死んだ。

一紀はふすまを開けとなりの部屋を見た。そこにはだれもいなかった。じつはそこに清右衛門の女房が病気のため寝ていたのであったが、一紀には蒲団の中の人間が目に入らなかった。表の方では、ひとびとの叫び声、わめき声がしていた。あちこちの部屋から女や客も出てきていた。一紀は血にまみれた刀をもち、ひとの声のする表の方へ引返していった。その時途中の急な階段から、階下の叫びを聞いて女郎のきしがころげるように降りてきた。一紀は階段の横から待ちぶせるようにしてそのきしの首めがけて刀を思い切り振りおろした。首は半分落ちかかるくらいに斬られ、きしは即死した。

そのあとから、女郎のしかが降りてきたが、頭と肩を斬られて倒れた。二階からは、女たちのあとからつづいて男三人が重なるように降りてきた。最初の男は右腕と尻に深い刀疵を受けて倒れ、次の男は顔と背中、三人目は左手首を斬り落されて、いずれも重傷を負うて倒れた。

二倒れた人間を足で払いのけるようにして一紀が表口の方までできてみると、そこにはだれもいなかった。階段下で、一瞬のうちに人が斬られる様を見て、部屋から飛び出してきた者はどこかに逃げたのだった。

12. 子飼（子飼い）apprentice trained from childhood.　妓楼としては全盛の時であった as a pleasure house, [Aburaya] was at its peak. *The sentence implies that it could have prospered even more as an oil merchant.*　難をまぬがれた（免れた）evaded, or was saved from, the disaster.　それにしても六十人もいる人間のほとんどがどこへ逃げたのかいないのだった even so (i.e., given that Seiemon was out that day), the fact is that nearly all of the remainder of the household amounting to sixty people were not there, having fled to no one knew where.　おこんに「まわし」をさせるほど客が多かったはずなのに despite the fact that there supposedly were so many patrons that [the manager] had to have Okon move from patron to patron.　斬られた三人のほかはどこへ消えうせたのか though no one knew where those [many patrons] excepting the three that were slain had vanished to.　少なくとも一紀には at least to Ikki.　ひとの気配は感じられなかった no sign of people being there was felt; there was no perceptible sign of people having been there.

13. 一紀が返り血でぬれた（濡れた）姿で立っているところ the spot where Ikki stood dripping with blood from those he had wounded or killed. 返り血 is blood spurting out from the victim, staining the attacker.　刀を受けとっていた場所 the place where he had taken his sword [back from Mano].　羽織もあずけてあった he had given [Mano] his kimono jacket for safekeeping [as well as his sword].　さすがに、その時の一紀は羽織のことは忘れていた as might well be expected, Ikki at that moment had forgotten about his jacket. *Ikki would have ordinarily remembered his jacket; but under the circumstances, he did not.*　重いものをぶらさげるようにもって holding [his sword] as if letting something heavy hang from his hand.　そのあとはわからなかった he was not himself after that; this was all he remembered.

14. どこかで刀が手から離れ his sword having left his hand at some place. *An unusual use of the sword as the subject implies that Ikki was unaware of when he let it fall.*　すでに手ぶらであった he had already been empty-handed. すでに、*used emphatically here, indicates that Ikki had been swordless for some time before he realized it.*　つい先程ひとが殺されたからだということはわかっていた at least he knew that [the reason he was walking in the dark] was because some people had been killed just a while ago. *The passive voice here is important. Ikki does not seem to have a sense that he is the one who killed them.*　なぜこうも急いで、暗やみを歩いているか why he was walking with such haste in the dark.　あそこへいって、ただ、少々酒をくらっただけではなかったか didn't he go to that place and merely drink a small amount of sake?

当時の油屋は、女郎三十八人、料理人三人、下女二人、下男三人、子飼十二人、主人夫婦、主人の母親、の六十一人の大家族で、妓楼としては全盛の時であった。事件の当日、主人清右衛門は、親戚の不幸のため外出して難をまぬがれたが、それにしても六十人もいる人間のほとんどがどこへ逃げたのかいないのだった。おこんに「まわし」をさせるほど客が多かったはずなのに、その多くの客は、斬られた三人の他はどこへ消えうせたのか、とにかく、一紀が表まで出てきた時、そこにはだれもいなかった。少なくとも一紀にはひとの気配は感じられなかった。

一紀が返り血でぬれた姿で立っているところは、つい先程万乃から刀を受けとっていた場所であった。万乃には、羽織もあずけてあった。しかし、さすがに、その時の一紀は羽織のことは忘れていた。右手の刀が重くなり、それを見ると血がついていた。その刀を、重いものをぶらさげるようにもって外へ出た。そのあとはわからなかった。

暗闇の中を、一紀は歩いていた。どこかで刀が手から離れ、すでに手ぶらであった。どこを、どっちの方角へ歩いているのか不明であった。ただ、自分が暗闇の中を歩いているのは、つい先程ひとが殺されたからだということはわかっていた。それは自分とはかかわりない事柄に感じられた。それより、なぜこうも急いで、暗闇を歩いているかの方が、不思議に思えるのだった。あそこへいって、ただ、少々酒をくらっただけではないか。満足のいくほども飲んでいないではないか。酒も思った

いったいあそこへなにをしにいったのか what on earth did he go there for? 思い出したように as if he remembered something (or what he was supposed to be doing). 圧縮された闇の間を押し割っていくように as if [the mountain trail at night stretched] forcefully, splitting the compressed space of darkness.

15. さらにやや東へ further somewhat eastward. 三里余の道 the route of over three *ri*. *Ri* as a unit of length differed widely from era to era and region to region. A length approximately 2.44 miles (3.9 kilometers) was used in the Edo period in Kansai and became nationally standardized in early Meiji. 明け方 at dawn. 生家で家を継ぎ百姓をしているのは弟の与三右衛門であった the one who succeeded to the family trade and worked as a cultivator at Ikki's native home was his younger brother Yosōemon. *As the older of the two, Ikki would have succeeded to the farm, had he stayed home. The next sentence notes that Ikki had not visited home for over a dozen years, hinting at his adoption into a different family.* 異様な風体に驚き入る taken aback by the strange appearance [of his older brother]. まるで他人事のように 話して聞かせた Ikki narrated [the event at Aburaya] as if it had happened to someone else. 叫びそうになるのをこらえていた restrained himself from being about to scream. と与三右衛門はいうのがやっとだった saying this was all Yosōemon could manage; he barely managed to say this. 血しぶき spurt of blood. 黒く固まり、ちぢんでいた had coagulated darkly and was shrunken. 黒い血の固まりのこびりついた、鳶色縮緬の袷 lined brown silk-crepe kimono caked with dark blood. 鳶 is a (black-eared) kite, 鳶色 tea-brown. 袷, a lined robe; cf. 単衣 (ひとえ), an unlined robe. 木綿の鼠小紋で裏は木綿のつぎつぎの袷 cotton kimono with *komon*-patterns on gray background with a lining of patched cotton. *Komon* refers to textile pattern of fine dots made from stencils and paste-resist, and also fabrics with such patterns. It was particularly popular in the Edo period.

16. どこへいくんだ、しばらくここに Where am I to go, let me stay here for a while. まもなくここへ追っ手がくるのがわからないのか don't you understand that the pursuers will be here soon? 学問をしたというのに、それしきのことがわからないのか you are a man of learning, and you don't understand such a simple thing? それしき, like たったそれぐらい or たったそればかり, means that the nature, content, or degree of a matter is insignificant. 今は他人でも、必ず疑われる though you are now a stranger to us, [as former immediate relatives] we are bound to be suspected. かかわりない他人のことで疑われるのは for us to be suspected because of [the conduct of] a total stranger. 迷惑千万 a great nuisance (a fixed phrase).

ほど飲まず、女も抱かずに、いったいあそこへなにをしにいったのか。一紀は、思い出したようにし

ばらく走り、また歩く。夜の山道は、圧縮された闇の間を押し割っていくように一紀に感じられた。

古市間の山から南へ山を越え、さらにやや東へ、三里余の道を一紀は歩き、松尾村畑茶屋の生家に

明け方たどりついた。生家で家を継ぎ百姓をしているのは弟の与三右衛門であった。十数年ぶりに会

う兄の異様な風体に驚きいる与三右衛門に、一紀は油屋での出来事を、まるで他人事のように話して

聞かせた。与三右衛門は、一紀の話しを聞きながら震え、叫びそうになるのをこらえていた。「ここ

にいてはいけない」と与三右衛門はいうのがやっとだった。「その、着物を脱いでくれ」と弟はいっ

た。三、四時間前に浴びた血しぶきは、黒く固まり、ちぢんでいた。一紀は、黒い血の固まりのこび

りついた、鳶色縮緬の袷を脱ぎ、弟の差し出す、木綿の鼠小紋で裏は木綿のつぎつぎの袷を着た。

「さあ、兄さん」と弟は着物を着がえた兄をうながした。

「どこへいくんだ、しばらくここに」と兄はいった。

「まもなくここへ追手がくるのがわからないのか兄さんは。兄さんは学問をしたというのに、それし

きのことがわからないのか。ここへは追手がくる。おれたちと兄さんとは今は他人でも、必ず疑われ

る。かかわりない他人のことで疑われるのは迷惑千万」と弟はいい、疲れはてた兄を追いたてる。

一紀が生家へ帰ったのは十数年ぶりであった。十歳のころに、鳥羽藩のさむらいの家から乞われて

17. 鳥羽藩 Toba Domain on the Shima peninsula in today's eastern Mie prefecture. In the Muromachi period, Shima was under the strong influence of the Ise Shrine. Toba is also a place name in southern Kyōto. さむらい (侍 or 士). *Tomioka's use of the hiragana recalls the original meaning of the word, one who does the act of waiting [upon the lord], from* さぶらう *or* さむらう. 〜から乞われて solicited by 〜. 養父 foster father. 一紀本人のかかわれぬところで取り沙汰されていた [the adoption in both cases] was discussed where Ikki himself was unable to have a say / out of Ikki's hearing.

18. あんた a corrupt form of あなた, used for one's superiors in mid- to late Edo. Now used for one's juniors, it is considered impolite in Tōkyō but endearing in Kansai. ここにいて迷惑かけてもらっては困る I don't want you to stay here and cause us annoyance. ニワトリ (鶏). Animal and plant names are often written in katakana. 去んでくれ please leave (dialectal), from the obsolete 去ぬ (more commonly written 往ぬ).

19. 闇の中にうごめいていた影絵のように like a silhouette that moved about in the dark. うごめく (蠢く), a compound made of the mimesis うご and the suffix めく, means to wriggle or squirm. Among other examples of words ending in めく are きらめく (to twinkle), さざめく (to make joyful noises), わめく (to scream). 会わなかったことにする [I] will pretend that I haven't seen [you]; as far as I'm concerned, I haven't seen you. 頼むから I beg of you.

20. なぜ、ここから去らねばならないのか *Four sentences starting with this one form an internal monologue.* なんと十数年ぶりに帰った家ではないか believe it or not, hadn't he come home after over a dozen years? なんと adds emphasis to the surprise element of a statement. 去ね去ねと追いたてられている he was being hurried to leave. 去ね, now only dialectal, is the imperative form of 去ぬ.

養子となり、さらにそこから十五歳の時に、現在の養父福間貞知に乞われて福間家の養子となっていた。いずれの養子縁組も、一紀本人のかかわれぬところで取り沙汰されていた。

「兄さん、あんたは、ここの家の者ではないのだから、ここにいて迷惑かけてもらっては困る」と百姓の弟はまたいった。

ニワトリがその時鳴き出した。

「水となにか食いものを」と殺人者はいった。

「とにかく、ここにいてもらっては困る。家の者が起きる前に去んでくれ。兄さん、ここへくるのなら、どうして浦田町の家へ帰らなかったのか」と弟はいった。

急に空が明るくなり、家のまわりの景色が鮮明になった。その明るさの中で、一紀には昨夜の油屋での自分が闇の中にうごめいていた影絵のように思い出された。

「兄さん、去んでくれ。おれは、兄さんに会わなかったことにする。頼むから、ここから去んでくれ」と弟は繰り返す。

ふいに、一紀は、弟のいっていることがわからなくなる。なぜ、ここから去らねばならないのか。なんと十数年ぶりに帰った家ではないか。その家へ帰ったとたんに、去ね去ねと追いたてられている。なぜここにいてはいけないのだろうか。

21. 中に入れまいとして弟が立ちふさがる家の奥には inside the house, to which his brother prevented him access.　自首する to give oneself up to the police.

22. 一刻も早く as soon as possible. 刻 is a unit of time obtained by (1) dividing the twenty-four hour period of day and night into 12 or 48 equal parts (also 50, 96, 100, or 120 for specific purposes) ; or (2) dividing day and night each into 6 or 18 equal units, unevenly balanced between day and night according to the season. In the Edo period, the latter was common.　お互いだれがだれとわからなかった [Ikki and anyone he encountered] would not know who the other was (だれがだれ *lit.*, who was whom).　利発だというだけで simply because he was bright. 百姓のせがれ(伜、倅)でなくなっていた [Ikki, as a child,] had no longer been a peasant's son.　並はずれて uncommonly.　養家 adoptive family.

23.　三里余りの道、しかも山越えの道 a path over three *ri*, a path across the mountains at that.　あの村から更に東へすすみ、古市、伊勢からなぜ 少しで も遠ざからなかったか why he did not go further eastward from that village (i.e., his native home, 松尾村) to distance himself as much as possible from Furuichi and Ise. *This semi-indirect narration passage should be read with attention to the use of* あの *and* そこ／その. *As Ikki goes over in his mind what happened searching for an explanation, the word* あの *is repeatedly used to refer to what he recalls:* あの 村、あの闇の中の影絵のような出来事、あの夜、あの坂、 あの中居. *Right after something has been referred to, the grammar requires* そ-*pronouns instead:* 坂の 上-その; 大楼があった-そこへ; 女がきた-その女; 刀を受けとった-その刀. むやみに immoderately, irresistibly.　だれかに説明 してもらい、納得したい Ikki wanted someone to explain [what it was all about] so he could understand (or: feel satisfied).

「父は？母は？」と一紀はいう。

「兄さん、とにかく帰ってくれ」と弟は同じことを繰り返すだけである。中に入れまいとして弟が立ちふさがる家の奥には、老いた父母がいるはずだった。

「兄さん、ひと時も早く自首してくれ」と弟はいった。

一紀は無言で家から離れ、一刻も早く村から離れようと足早に歩いた。知ったひとにはだれにも会わなかった。もし会っていたとしても、一紀もその人間もお互いだれがだれとわからなかった。子供の一紀は利発だというだけで百姓のせがれでなくなっていた。並はずれて利発というだけで養家では可愛がられた。

三里余りの道、しかも山越えの道を、一紀はまた引き返そうとしていた。もう一度きた道を戻ろうとしているのだった。ただし今度は朝の光の中を歩いている。これからどこへいくのか、一紀本人にもわかっていない。なぜまた、元へ戻ろうとするのかわからない。あの村から更に東へすすみ、古市、宇治からなぜ少しでも遠ざからなかったかわからない。ただ、むやみに、一紀はだれかに逢いたいのである。自分を知るだれかに逢って、あの闇の中の影絵のような出来事がなんだったか説明してもらいたいのだ。自分が説明できるわけがない。自分はただやったことしかわからない。それがいったいなんだったかだれかに説明してもらい、納得したい。あの夜、間の山への

人殺しの声の中で amidst the voices that called out "murder!"

24. 濃い闇のかたまりの中へ首をつっこんでいくような気がしていた he had felt as if he were thrusting his head further and further into the thick mass of darkness.　坂を上っていくにしたがって(従って) as he went up the hill.　あかり(明かり、明り、灯) lights.　それらをくぐりぬけているのに 見えていたものが見えなくなるのだった despite the fact that he was making his way through an increasingly well-lit area, what had been visible to him was (contrariwise) becoming invisible. *This passage in semi-indirect narration is studded with paradoxical statements like darkness in the lighted street, heavy-heartedness as a result of thrilling joy, an almost depressing pleasure, and gloomy humor.*　見かけとは逆に contrary to appearances.　自分を知るひとはだれも知らぬ not a single person who knew Ikki knew [that he was drinking alone in a small Aburaya room].　かれらのどこにもいない (*lit.*) Ikki existed in no part of them; Ikki might as well not have existed for them.　その痛快さを抑えるのに気が重いくらいだった he was almost heavy-hearted in suppressing that keen pleasure; it was so thrilling to feel that way (i.e., to feel he did not exist in their consciousness) that it made him heavy-hearted as he tried to suppress that feeling.

長いあの坂をふと登っていったのはなに事だったのか。坂の上の両側に女郎屋が並んでいた。その
いちばんの高所に油屋という大楼があった。思いついたようにそこへあがった。仲居に羽織と刀をあ
ずけた。女がきた。その女が呼ばれて出ていった。ひとりで酒を飲んだ。帰りがけにあの仲居から刀
を受けとった。その刀を抜いたら仲居の指が斬れた。それから人殺しの声の中で人を殺していた。
「人殺し」の声があがり、その声の中へ入っていって人を殺していた。そこまでしか一紀にはわから
ない。

　二四
　あの長い急な坂を登っていった時、不思議に濃い闇のかたまりの中へ首をつっこんでいくような気
がしていたのを一紀は思いかえした。坂を登っていくにしたがって、両側に並ぶ妓楼や商家のあかり
がふえ、それらをくぐりぬけているのに見えなくなるのだった。坂を登り切った時、
闇のかたまりの中に自分が浮んでいるように思えた。その気分は、見かけとは逆に、一紀を機嫌よく
させていた。闇の中に浮んでいる自分が、次第に闇の中に溶けていくのだった。自分もなにも見えな
いけど、自分も他人から見えないにちがいない。今、自分が、油屋の小部屋で、ひとり酒を飲んでい
るのは、だれも知らない。養父も知らぬ。自分を知るひとはだれも知らぬ。自分は今、かれらのどこ
にもいない。その痛快さを抑えるのに気が重いくらいだった。だれも知らないところにいるのは、自
分が消えてしまっていることと同じではないか。自分はここにいる。しかし、自分を知る者はだれも

それなのに、その気のめいる(滅入る)ほどの愉快を放擲してなぜあの時立ち あがったのか why, then, had he risen to his feet, abandoning the pleasure that almost depressed him?　そういえば come to think of it. *Ikki's thought returns from the Aburaya event to his present status.*　頭を抱えてしゃがみこんでしま いたいほどに almost making him want to crouch with his head in his hands.　陰 気なおかしさ gloomy humor; somber comicality.　からだの底からせり上が ってくる pushing up from the core of his body. せり上がる, to rise powerfully from below, is also a term used in kabuki for an actor to rise from the pit by a stage device.

25. 大夫 originally, the fifth rank and higher at court. The title came to be used for an Ise Shintō office called *gon no negi* (see below) because that position was regarded as equal to the fifth courtly rank. 大夫 is also pronounced たゆう, だゆう, だいぶ depending upon what it refers to.　御師 short for 御祷師 (おいのりし), a Buddhist priest or Shintō official who offers prayers at the request of his adherents/parishioners in exchange for a fee. The last half of this paragraph explains the term further.　御師職 the office of *oshi*, or a person who holds the office.　祈祷 師 one who offers prayers professionally.　伊勢参宮者 visitors to the Ise Shrine. 宿泊の世話をし、参宮の案内もする祈祷師と旅館業を兼ねており combined the professions of praying and inn-keeping by accommodating visitors and giving guided tours of the shrines.　神宮の正員の補宜の家柄を最高に headed by the *negi* family that is a member of a shrine. 神宮 is a Shintō shrine, especially of a high rank. 補宜 literally means "one who comforts the gods," from the archaic verb ねぐ (to comfort).　権補宜 assistant *negi*. The word 権 means temporary or second-rank and is prefixed to the name of an office.　五位の位 the fifth court rank.　五位の唐名 the Chinese name for the fifth rank.

26. そこへはゆかず (行かず) instead of going there [to his adoptive father's home]. ゆかず is a slightly archaic negative form of ゆく.　藤浪家 the Fujinami house. The name recalls 藤波 (ふじなみ), a historical Shintō official family in Tsushma in Owari province.　神宮家といわれる御師の最高の階級の家 the highest-rank *oshi* house called the Shrine house.　福間大夫の主筋にあたること になる it follows that the Fujinami house was a master house in relation to Fukuma Taifu.

27. すでに捕手が待ちかまえていると [judging] that the pursuers were already on the lookout for him.　しのび (忍び) 入った stole in.　養父福間大夫より も、藤浪神主のほうがはるかに土地の有力者だから because Fujinami was a far greater local power than his stepfather Fukuma, (it would be advantageous to go

今自分がここにいるのを知らぬ。それなのに、その気のめいる程の愉快を放擲してなぜあの時立ちあがったのか。そういえば、今こうして、太陽が天の真上にある真昼に、自分が山の中にいるのもだれひとり知らない。そう思うと、頭をかかえてしゃがみこんでしまいたいほどに一紀に陰気なおかしさがからだの底からせり上ってくるのが感じられた。

一紀の養父福間貞知は大夫と呼ばれる御師であった。御師とは御師職、つまり祈祷師のことであるが、当時、伊勢参宮者の宿泊の世話をし、参宮の案内もする祈祷師と旅館業を兼ねており、相当な暮しをする者もあった。御師には四階級があり、神宮の正員の禰宜の家柄を最高に、権禰宜の家がその次であった。この権禰宜は多くが五位の位をもっており、大夫と呼ばれていた。それは五位の唐名が大夫なので、そこからきていた。一紀の養父はこの地位の御師であった。

養父の屋敷のある浦田町までできた一紀は、そこへはゆかず、藤浪家の屋敷へ入っていった。藤浪家は禰宜の家柄の御師で、神宮家といわれる御師の最高の階級の家であった。一紀の養父福間大夫の主筋にあたることになる。

福間大夫の家には、すでに捕手が待かまえていると、一紀は判断して藤浪邸へしのび入ったのだろうか。その判断より、養父福間大夫よりも、藤浪神主のほうがはるかに土地の有力者だからとの直感がはたらいていたからではないか。神宮家である藤浪神主は、土地の政経の両面でハバをきかせて

to the latter's house). The term 神主 here means a chief official who supervises all Shintō events, rather than a Shintō official in general. In the following passages, Fujinami is referred to as 長官, chief or head official.   ～との直感がはたらいていたからではないか perhaps his intuition had told him that ～.   政経の両面 both aspects of politics and economy.   ハバ（幅）をきかせて（利かせて）いた made his influence felt; 幅を利かす is synonymous with 羽振りを利かす, where *haburi* literally means the flapping or appearance of the wings. *Tomioka's use of katakana for* ハバ、アイマイ、ナワバリ *in this story calls attention to writing and narrating as constituted of selective and arbitrary choices by an author or storyteller.*

28. 丸一日 one whole day.   当惑 perplexity; annoyance.   一紀をかくまう（匿う）わけにはゆかぬ（行かぬ） it was impossible for them to shelter Ikki. ゆかぬ is another archaic negative form of ゆく.   座敷にあげた allowed him in to a tatami room. あげる, because of the raised-floor structure of a Japanese house. 家来らしき者 someone who appeared to be a subordinate. らしき, slightly archaic, makes the noun phrase tighter than らしい.

29. 長官におとりつぎください please let the head official know I am here. 二十歳にはならぬ息子 a son who was not yet 20. ならぬ is an archaic negative form of なる.

30. 引き渡していただきたい we request that you deliver him to us.   夜番の者 a night guard.   見知らぬ者 a stranger.

いた。

藤浪家にも一紀のことは伝えられていた。もうその時は事件から、丸一日たっていたから当然だった。

(二八) 一紀が邸内に入ったことを知らされた藤浪家のひとたちの当惑は大きかった。一紀をかくまうわけにはゆかぬ。しかしとにかく一紀を座敷にあげた。

「昨夜、油屋で——」と一紀がいいかけると、「なぜ福間大夫のところに帰らぬか」と藤浪神主の家来らしき者がいった。

(二九) 一紀はひとりで放っておかれた。「長官におとりつぎ下さい」と一紀は何度か家来にいったが藤浪家の家の者は姿を見せなかった。まだ二十歳にはならぬ息子がいるのを一紀は知っていたが、その息子の姿もなかった。

(三〇) 最初に出てきた家来らしき者が戻ってきたので、一紀は「福間大夫のところに戻る」といった。すると、その男は、「ここから出てはならぬ」といい、また奥へ消えた。

その時、表の方で声が聞えた。「ここへ福間一紀が入ったと知らせた者がある、もしそれが真実なら引き渡していただきたい」とだれかがいっている。

「そんなはずはない、門には夜番の者がいます。見知らぬ者はこの邸内へは入れない」と先の家来ら

31. やはりかくまうつもりだと [Ikki thought] that, as expected, the Fujinami intended to shelter him.　なんという恩知らず what an ingrate.　大夫があれほど嫌う間の山で at Ai no Yama (where the pleasure quarters are located) that your foster father hates so much. *This first mention of the strong feeling of Ikki's foster father alludes to his Shintoist purism on the surface and also foreshadows a later revelation of his secret love for his son.*　女と遊び、酒を飲んでの人殺し murder after, or on the spur of, having enjoyed women and drunk sake.　どうやら神主からいわれた通りに述べたてる stated eloquently, as he more or less seemed.

32. だから、大夫のところに帰ると— so I am telling you I will go back to my foster father's place.　いや、ここからは出せぬ no, we can't let you leave this place. 出せぬ is the archaic negative of 出す.　藤波の家にいたことがわかっては if it becomes known [to the authorities] that you have been here.　詫びねばならない I have to apologize [to my foster father].　それではここにしばらく if that is the case, let me stay here for a while.　振り払うように as if to shake off [Ikki's words].　自害されるように please take your own life. *Here and later in this passage, the Fujinami servant's tone is polite with the use of honorifics.*　つき（突き）放した thrust away, tossed off; i.e., Ikki repeated his plea to see Fujinami, but the subordinate brushed it off, saying he was not home.

しき者が答えている。

「夜番を呼べ」という声が遠ざかる。

一紀が藤浪家に入る時夜番はいなかった。家来らしき者の答を聞いて、やはりかくまうつもりだと一紀は思った。福間大夫の家に帰る気持ははじめからなかった。

「なんという恩知らず。福間大夫がお前に学問させ、京都に留学させてくれたのを忘れたのか。大夫の嘆きを考えないのか。大夫があれほど嫌う間の山で、女と遊び、酒を飲んでの人殺し。かくまうわけにはいかない」と家来らしき者は、どうやら神主からいわれた通りに述べたてる。

「だから、大夫のところに帰ると──」と一紀はいった。

「いや、ここからは出せぬ。藤浪の家にいたことがわかっては、この家は迷惑する」

「大夫に詫びねばならない」と一紀はいったが、なにを詫びるのかわからなかった。

「家のまわりには捕手がかこんでいる。ここからは出さない」と家来らしき者は繰り返す。

「それではここにしばらく──」と一紀がいうのを振り払うように、「自害されるように」と家来らしき者はいい、それは藤浪神主の命令だとつけ加えた。

「藤浪神主に会わせていただきたい」と一紀はいったが、「長官はおられない」と家来らしき者はつき放した。

とにかく、長官から自害されるようにとのこと anyway, the directive from the chief official requests that you take your life.　　自首ではなく自害せよとは、といぶかった（訝った）Ikki wondered why he was told not to surrender to the police but to commit suicide.

33. 妻帯 being married to a woman.　　二十七歳にして (*literary*) at age twenty-seven.　　特異 unusual.　　容姿 appearance.　　申し分ない男子 a man about whom one could say nothing critical.　　養父がそれをのぞまぬからであった [the reason that Ikki was not married] was that his stepfather did not want it. *This and the next sentence, indicating that Ikki did not understand well why his stepfather wished him (Ikki) to remain single, hint at the nature of the father's fondness for Ikki.*

34. 大小の刀 a pair of swords, one long and one short. *Ikki is ordered to commit suicide the samurai way.*　　いずれ命はないのだから you can't escape death one way or another.　　自害された方が福間大夫も苦しみから解かれる your committing suicide would liberate your stepfather from his pains.　　そんなことをしたらこちらにもご迷惑になる if I did something like that (committing suicide here), it would cause trouble to the Fujinami house.　　まだ命乞いをされるのか do you still beg for your life?　　藤浪の家から出てはもらえぬ we cannot let you out of the Fujinami house.　　無理にでもしていただく [if you refuse to take your own life,] we will have you do so if necessary by force. *The language suggests that the Fujinami were determined at least nominally to have Ikki "commit suicide" (force Ikki to enact sham suicide) even as they probably intended to save his life.*　藤浪神主に話を聞いてもらうためにここに来たと—— I have come here to ask Fujinami to listen to what I have to say—please let him know.

「とにかく、長官から自害されるようにとのこと」と一紀はいわれたが、自首ではなく自害せよとは、まっといぶかった。養父福間大夫も自首ではなく自害せよというだろうか。ただ養父に会いたいとはまったく考えなかった。

三三　福間大夫は妻帯していなかった。二十七歳の一紀もまたまだ妻帯していなかった。二十七歳にして妻のないことは当時としては特異であった。一紀は家柄、職業、学問、容姿、どれも申し分ない男子であるのに妻帯していないのは、養父がそれをのぞまぬからであった。なぜ養父が一紀の妻帯をのぞまぬかを、一紀本人はよくわからなかった。

三四　藤浪神主の家来らしき者がしばらくしてまたあらわれ、大小の刀を一紀のかたわらに置いた。「いずれ命はないのだから、自害された方が福間大夫も苦しみから解かれる。さあ、早く」と家来らしき者はいった。

「自害するためにここにきたのではない。そんなことをしたらこちらにもご迷惑になる」と一紀はいった。

「まだ命乞いをされるのか。おわかりにならないのか。藤浪の家から出てはもらえぬ。自害していただきたい。もし、いやだといわれるなら、無理にでもしていただく」

「藤浪神主に話を聴いてもらうためにここにきたと──」

長官に命乞いを願うというのは筋ちがい it's wrong for you to plead with Fujinami for your life; you have come to the wrong person.　In Edo 筋違いの願い
means bringing a suit to a court of the wrong jurisdiction.

35. 板敷きのところ wooden-floored space.　布を巻きつけた刀を握らせた
made [Ikki] hold in his hand a sword wrapped with cloth. *The wrapped sword indicates that Ikki is being forced to go through ritual suicide.*　着物の前を開いた
opened the front of Ikki's kimono (to expose his abdomen).　羽交い締めのよう
に as if to pinion [Ikki].　一紀のうしろから両手を まわして押さえていた
putting both arms around from behind Ikki, [the third man] held him still.　うしろ
にまわった男の一方の手が重なり one hand of the man in back was placed [over
Ikki's hand that was made to hold the sword].　その手は一紀の下腹で動いてい
た and that hand (i.e., the third man's) moved along Ikki's lower abdomen. *Along
with the use of the hand as the subject in the last sentence of the paragraph, the use
of-ていた in 押さえていた and 動いていた conveys a sense of detachment, as
with stage actions observed from an outsider's point of view. The three unidentified
men here recall bunraku puppeteers in black with covered faces. As three puppeteers manipulate one puppet, these three men manipulate Ikki and his "suicide."*
そこには先程一紀がいるか どうかを調べにきた役人が待っていた waiting
there was the officer who had come a while ago to check if Ikki was at the Fujina-
mis. *This suggests the officer had some kind of understanding about Ikki's suicide
play.*

36. 検使 a term used from Muromachi onward for officers dispatched to examine
the facts, especially of land disputes, unnatural deaths, and executions; also those
who observed ceremonial suicides.　役人六人連名で with the joint signatures of
six officers.
一　臍の下……
　　Item: A wound in one place under the navel, over 8 *sun* long and approxi-
　　mately 1.5 *sun* deep.
　　Item: A wound in one place on the throat, over 2 *sun* long and approximately
　　1.5 *sun* deep.
　　Item: In a lined cotton kimono with small patterns against a grey background
　　and a lining of cotton patches.
　　Item: Wore an amber-colored crepe sash.
　　Item: Absolutely nothing carried in his chest pockets.
　　Item: A sword, 23.8 *sun* long and inscribed "Kanetsune," etc.
　　Item: A short sword, 16.8 *sun* long and inscribed "Yoshimitsu of Osafune in
　　Bizen," etc.

「長官に命乞いを願うというのは筋ちがい」と家来らしき者がいううちに、いつの間にか三人の男が一紀のまわりにいた。

男たちは一紀をひきずるように、薄暗い板敷のところへつれていった。

男たちのひとりが一紀に布をまきつけた刀を握らせた。もうひとりが一紀の着物の前を開いた。三人目の男が、羽交締めのように一紀のうしろから両手をまわして押さえていた。刀を握らせられた一紀の手に、うしろにまわった男の一方の手が重なり、その手は一紀の下腹で動いていた。

家来らしき者が屋敷の表へ出ていった。そこには先程一紀がいるかどうかを調べにきた役人が待っていた。

五月七日の日付で検使役人六人連名で出された書類には次のように記されていた。

一　臍の下長さ八寸余深さ一寸五分斗の疵一ヶ所

一　咽喉長さ二寸余深さ一寸五分疵一ヶ所

一　木綿鼠　小紋裏木綿つぎ〳〵袷　着用

一　琥珀堅縮帯致し居り申候、

一　懐中もの　一切無之候

一　刀長二尺三寸八分銘兼常と有之云々

尺、寸、分 measurements of length. One *sun* is approximately 3.8 or 3 centimeters depending upon the standard. The latter became official in 1875. For convenience's sake it can be translated into "inch" in English. 10 *sun* make 1 *shaku*, and 10 *bu* make 1 *sun*.　堅縮（方縮）a type of crepe made with the use of strongly twisted thread for the woof.　致し居り申し候（いたしております），無之候（ございません），と有之（と書いてあり）typical expressions in *sōrōbun* (候文). *Sōrōbun* originated as a style for personal letters. In the Edo period it was also widely used in official letters. It continued to be the standard form for official correspondence until the end of WWII. This style of writing is characterized by the abundant use of the auxiliary verb 候, originally from a verb meaning "to wait in service," and by the occasional Chinese word order, especially in fixed phrases.　銘 inscription.　兼常 the name of a sword maker.　備前長船賀光 the name of a sword maker of the Osafune school. Osafune is a place name in Bizen (now Okayama prefecture). 云々 etc.

37.「自害した」一紀 Ikki who had supposedly committed suicide.　疵の手当てをされて having been treated for his wounds.　夜の闇をくぐりぬけて through the dark of the night. くぐりぬける（潜り抜ける），to go under and through [a difficult situation or a danger], implies a stealthy or speedy action.

38. よろめきもせず一紀を抱きかかえて holding Ikki in his arms without so much as reeling.　赤児をおくようにそうっとのせた placed [Ikki on the futon] gently as if putting down a baby.　死なせはしない no, [whatever else I may do] I will not let you die.　息子の腹に巻きつけられた布 cloth wrapping around his son's belly.　押しのけるように as if to shove away.　疵のありかを探した looked for wounds. ありか（在処）means a place where something is.　腹に疵はあるが、浅い疵に見えた there was a wound on the abdomen but it seemed shallow. *Fukuma's discovery of just a shallow wound on Ikki's abdomen and none on the throat, unlike in the official report, points to the fact that the three men who enacted the suicide scene had been instructed to inflect a light wound just for formality's sake. Suicide by seppuku, unassisted by a* kaishaku *(assistant) who severs the head, would have required stabbing the throat.*

39. 本来なら、一紀は生きておれぬ properly speaking, Ikki was in no position to escape death.　したがって藤浪神主が一紀の命を助けたことは福間大夫も承知している Fukuma knew, therefore, that Fujinami had spared Ikki's life. 無理強いに自害させられた [Ikki] was forcibly made to commit (sham) suicide.

一脇指長さ一尺六寸八分備前長船賀光と有之云々

ところが、一紀はその五月七日に死んでいなかった。

役人が「自害した」一紀を見たあと、一紀は疵の手当をされて福間大夫の家に夜の闇をくぐりぬけて運びこまれていた。

福間大夫はもう五十歳をかなり過ぎていたが、よろめきもせず一紀を抱きかかえて自分の部屋に運び、蒲団の上に赤児をおくようにそうっとのせた。

「死なせはしない」と父親はいった。

父親は、息子の腹に巻きつけられた布を押しのけるように開き、血の中に疵のありかをさがした。

腹に疵はあるが、浅い疵に見えた。首に疵はない。まだ夜は明けない。

福間大夫は勿論油屋での事件を知らされていた。ひとを二人殺し、数人がかなりの疵を負ったという。その後、疵を受けた者のひとりが死んだとも知らされていた。一紀は三人の人間を殺したことになる。本来なら、一紀は生きておれぬ。したがって藤浪神主が一紀の命を助けたことは福間大夫も承知している。それなのに福間大夫は納得がゆかない。一紀は無理強いに自害させられたのだという思いは消えないのである。もしも一紀が、藤浪の屋敷へ逃げこまず、この家に帰ってきていたら、と父親は何度も何度も思う。あの時はすでに、家のまわりには役人がいた。やはり藤浪の屋敷へ一紀がいっ

40. 大夫の耳から頭の奥をゆすぶるように [Ikki's groan rang] as if to rock Fukuma from his ears to the inside of his brain. 　十年は二人で 暮らしてきた they had lived together at least ten years. 　身のまわりから煮炊きの世話までしてくれた [Until Ikki left to study in Kyōto, he] had handled everything from Fukuma's care to cooking. 　家の使用人の 沸かす風呂にも大夫は入らないのだった Fukuma would not even bathe in the water heated by a servant; *i.e., he only liked the bath Ikki made.* 　女ひとりもおかなかった Fukuma did not keep even one woman servant. 　不浄の靄が立ちこめる気配がした [the presence of a woman] seemed to Fukuma to hint at a pervasive haze of impurity. *This paragraph also points to the nature of Fukuma's love for his foster son.*

41. 無理強いにつけられた疵 a wound that was forcibly made. 　そのことが大夫には解せぬ that was incomprehensible to Fukuma.

42. 逆上（ぎゃくじょう）の果てに as a result of losing himself to anger. 逆上, (*lit.*) a rush of blood to the head, means frenzy or losing one's wits. *The emphatic dots added to 逆上 point to Fukuma's strong response to the expression: in his view, Ikki was clever and composed since childhood, quietly playing the role his foster father assigned him; he was not one to lose his temper.*

たのはよかったのか。

四〇　疲れはててねむる一紀の、うめく声が大夫の耳から頭の奥をゆすぶるように響いている。

福間大夫が美しく賢い少年一紀と出会ってから、十年以上になる。その間、一紀の京都留学の三年をのぞいても、十年はふたりで暮してきた。京都へ留学するまで、この一紀が身のまわりから煮炊きの世話までしてくれたのが大夫はまるで遠い思い出のように感じられた。家の使用人の沸かす風呂にも大夫は入らないのだった。家の中には女ひとりもおかなかった。福間大夫には、女がいるということは、そこに不浄の靄が立ちこめる気配がした。

四一　藤浪神主は一紀の命を助けてくれた。それならばなぜ、一紀に疵をつけずにこの父親に返してくれなかったかと、大夫はまだ納得がいかない。たしかに、腹の疵は、申し訳程度の浅い疵だ。しかし、その疵は、無理強いにつけられた疵だ。そのことが大夫には解せぬ。

四二　油屋の出来事を知らせた者は、一紀が女を待ちくたぶれ、逆上のはてに人を殺したといった。

「逆上」はせぬ、一紀は」と大夫はふいに大声をあげた。

四三　それにしても、一紀は油屋からここへなぜすぐに馳けこんでこなかったのか、と大夫は思う。四日の真夜中から五日にかかる事件である。一紀が藤浪の屋敷に入ったのは六日の夜、この家に運ばれたのが七日になってからというのも福間大夫はわからない。なぜ油屋からまっすぐここへこなかったの

43. 自分を避けたからだ [that Ikki did not return to Fukuma's house] was because Ikki had avoided him.　避けたのではない、嫌ったのだと大夫はみずから訂正する Ikki did not avoid me but [rather] took a dislike of me, Fukuma corrected himself.　いや、嫌うというよりも no, it's less that Ikki dislikes me than....　言葉で改まらぬ [he started correcting himself once again but] it was not verbally revised, i.e., he was unable to verbalize his thought.

44. 父親にさからった（逆らった）ことはなかった [Ikki] had never defied his father.　信じがたい（難い）hard to believe, incredible.　元通りにはゆかなくなった [after his return from Kyōto] things were not the same.　反感 antipathy.　嫌悪 hatred.　どこかが食いちがっていた something was wrong.　そのどこかというものをたぐると when they traced back to that something. たぐる（手繰る）means to pull (a string) hand over hand.　そうすることで by doing so, i.e., concealing that there was "woman" (the opposite sex) at the source of their estrangement and that they had different perceptions of "woman."　辛うじて一紀の嗅いでいる「女」のにおいに対する嫉妬のごとき感情を抑えており [Fukuma] barely managed to suppress a feeling like jealousy toward the smell of "woman" that Ikki was taking in.　養父のかなしみ（悲しみ）に触れなかった [and by doing the same, Ikki] refrained from touching his foster father's sorrow.

45. 昨六日の夜……(mod. J.:) 昨日六日の夜、私どもの家において福間一紀が 自害いたしました始末について、お尋ねでございます。昨日の夜、一番鶏のなくころ、家来のものが来て申しますには、一紀がこの町へ入り込んだとかで、町内が騒ぎ立てているとのことでした。そこで早速近辺のものや家来などを呼びにやり、境内を見回らせ、なおまた座敷などを見回らせましたところ、座敷中通りの板の間に、一紀はすでに自害をしておりました。驚いて、早速そのよしを長官へ告げにやりましたところ、「もし大小などがそばにあったら、取りのけておくように」と言ってよこしましたので、取り上げておき、前のとおり長官からお役所へ申しあげました。そこでご検使役がいろいろにお調べなさいました。ご見分のとおり、一紀が自害を致しましたことにまちがいはございません。

The authorities have inquired into the circumstances in which Fukuma Ikki committed suicide at our house last night on the sixth. Last night, around the time of the first cock's crow, a servant reported to me that Ikki seemed to have entered our town and that the townspeople were making a great fuss. So without delay we sent for those nearby and family servants, and had them search within the complex and also the tatami rooms, whereupon, Ikki was found to have already committed suicide on the wooden floor between tatami spaces. Surprised, we sent word to Head Official Fujinami. We were then told to put aside Ikki's swords if he wore a pair, so

か。それは逆上のゆえなのか。一紀は逆上していなかった、今まで少年の日から一紀は一度も逆上などしたことはない。一紀は逆上するような男ではない、と養父は自分にいいきかせるようにいう。油屋からここに帰らなかったのは、自分を避けたからだと大夫は思う。避けたのではない、嫌ったのだと大夫はみずから訂正する。いや、嫌うというより、ともう一度訂正しかけるが、言葉で改まらぬ。

父親は息子の口に水をこぼすように少しずつそそいでやる。

四四　一紀は今まで一度も父親にさからったことはなかった。京都留学も一紀が申し出たのではなく、大夫のすすめに従ったのであった。一紀は、三年もの間、大夫の手元から離されるのが信じがたいほどであった。しかし、京都から帰ってのちは、元通りにはゆかなくなった。大夫への反感でも嫌悪でもなかった。どこかが食いちがっていた。その、どこかというものをたぐると、それが「女」だというのに、大夫も一紀も気はついていた。「女」に対する感覚がすでに離れていた。それを、ふたりはかくしつづけていた。大夫はそうすることで、辛うじて一紀の嗅いでいる「女」のにおいに対する嫉妬のごとき感情を抑えており、一紀はそうすることで養父のかなしみに触れなかった。

四五　藤浪家は、五月七日の日付で、役人に宛てて一紀の事件についての届を出している。

「昨六日の夜私宅に於て福間一紀自害仕り候　始末御尋ねに御座候　昨夜鶏鳴頃家来の者申し来り候、

we took them away. Then, the Head Official reported to the government office as he did, and the officers made their inspection. There is no doubt that Ikki had committed suicide just as the examination revealed.
と届けの最初にある　this is what appears at the beginning of the report.

46. そのことからすでになにやらおかしい　that [the report was submitted under the joint names of the daughter, son, wife, mother, and relatives' representative, without Fujinami's name] was already somewhat suspicious. おかしい　here means odd or suspicious, not amusing.　いかにも無理がある　[the text of the report] was illogical no matter how one looks at it.　わざわざことわっている　[the report] deliberately stated [that the case was unmistakably a suicide as made clear by the inspection].　不在ではないはずである　[the head official Fujinami] could not have been absent (since his involvement in the incident is described in the report).　一紀の「自害」なるを認めさせたれたと受けとれる　it could be understood that [the examiners] were compelled to acknowledge the fact of Ikki's having committed suicide, i.e., they were forced to accept Fujinami's claim due to his powerful status.　偽装ではないかと思わせる　[the situation] made one think that Ikki's suicide might have been a sham / camouflage.

47. 次のようなもってまわった説明を加える必要がない　there would have been no need to add [to the report] such a roundabout explanation as follows. 届の後半に曰く　it says in the last half of the report.
尤私共……(mod. J.:) もっとも、私どもが寝ておりましたところから、一紀が自害いたしました場所へは、部屋の数も多く、へだたって居りました。この一紀はどこから入ったのでしょうか。いろいろ調べましたところ、表門は平日番人がかんぬきをさしておりますので、くぐり戸は夜分でも開けておきますが、外から内へは、入るところがございません。ところが、夜番のものが便所へ行っておりました間に、その時入ったかと存じます。それにまた、今朝、明け方に牛谷というものがまいりまして、一紀がこちらへ入ったよしを聞いたとのことで、身柄を渡すよう告げました。そこへ家来の片岡政右衛門が出てまいり、「長官へ知らせるからしばらく待つように」と申し、一紀がすでに自害していることも申しませんでした。これでは一紀をかくまっているかのようで、全く政右衛門の心得違いであり、私ども恐れ入るしだいでございます。上記の一紀が帰ってきたということで町内が騒ぎ立てましたら、早速起きだして、家の中の取締など、注意すべきところ、手遅れになりました。その上、一紀が自害しておりますなら早速家来をつけておき、あれこれ注意すべきでしたが、長官から指図があるまで手延べにしておりました。不行き届き・取りはからい不調法のいたりであり、恐れ入ります。なおまた、せがれの勘解由は年が若く、その他のものどもは女であり、ことに距離も隔

は一紀儀当町へ入り込候 趣 にて町内相騒ぎ候 段申来り候 に付早速近辺の者家来等呼ひに遣はし境見まはらせ尚又座敷をも見廻らせ候 ところ座敷中通板の間に自害仕 り罷り在り候 打驚き早速其段長官へ申し達し候 処大小等側に有之候 はゞ取退け置き候 様申越し候に付取上げ前の通長官より御役所へ申し上候 処各 様御検使成せられ御見分の通り自害仕 候 に相違無之候 」と届の最初にある。

四六

　この届は藤浪神主の娘、息子、妻、母、親戚代表の連名で出されていて、藤浪長官の名はない。そのことからすでになにやらおかしい。届の文章には、いかにも無理がある。検使の通り自害に相違ないとわざわざことわっている。一紀が自害し、それを検使役人が調べたのであれば、改めてそんなことをいう必要はなく、ただ、福間一紀なる者が自害し、検使の役人が確認したといえばいい。それに、長官は一紀の自害を知らされ、大小の刀を取退けておけと命じ、またすぐ役所へ申出ているのだから不在ではないはずである。検使役人が、藤浪長官に、一紀の「自害」が擬装ではないかと思わせる。いや、受けとれるのでなく、一紀の「自害」なるを認めさせられたと受けとれる。

四七

　また、擬装でなければ届に次のようなもってまわった説明を加える必要がない。

　後半に曰く——「尤 私 共臥居候 処より自害仕 り候 場所へ間数も隔 居り申し候 右一紀儀何れ

たっているという事情でございまして、なにがなにやら一向にわきまえませ
んでした。よって、このよし、お役人に申し上げます。以上

However, there was a distance of many rooms from where we were sleeping to where the suicide took place. Where had the above-mentioned Ikki entered? As we investigated in various ways [it was clarified that] because the guard keeps the front gate bolted on normal days, even though the wicket door is open even at night, from outside there is no way to enter the house. This being the case, we conjecture that, as the guard had gone to the toilet, Ikki then entered. Again, one by the name of Ushitani came over at dawn today and told us that he had heard that Ikki had entered our complex and that we should deliver Ikki. But Kataoka Seiemon, our subordinate, appeared and told Ushitani to wait for a while since we were sending word to Fujinami; yet he did not even mention that Ikki had committed suicide. This may have sounded as if sheltering Ikki. It was wholly Seiemon's error, for which we accept the blame. If townspeople made a commotion about the above-mentioned Ikki having returned, we should have promptly risen and examined security inside the house and so forth, but we were too slow. Moreover, if Ikki had committed suicide, we should have posted our retainers there and paid attention to all matters, but we waited until Fujinami gave instructions. For this lack of care and clumsy handling, we are sorry. Further, because Fujinami's son Kageyu is young and the rest of us are women, and particularly because we were separated by a long distance, we had no idea at all as to what was happening. Thus, we report this to the authorities. The end.

48. 〜というのはいいとして accepting that 〜.　牛谷なる役人と思われる者 one by the name of Ushitani who seemed to be an officer.　待たせておいて while [Seiemon] had [Ushitani] wait.　いつの間にか侵入して自害していた、それを言わずに without stating the crucial fact that Ikki had entered and committed suicide before anyone realized it.　一紀をかくまっていたかのごとく（如く）にいったのは the fact that [Seiemon] spoke as if they were sheltering Ikki.　いかにもいい訳がましい sounds precisely like an excuse.　その間に、一紀に偽装の自害をさせたととれる it can be inferred that, in the meantime, they made Ikki perform a sham suicide.

49. 奉行所 the magistrate's office. In the Edo period, there were three types of bugyō: *jisha bugyō*, *machi bugyō*, and *kanjō bugyō*, which handled, respectively, temples and shrines, city affairs, and finance. Here the term refers to *machi bugyō*. 阿州商人の由にて…… (*mod. J.*:) 阿波の国の商人とかで、同じ町の大阪屋作右衛門のところに 泊まっていた伊太郎、岩二郎、孫三郎の三人の者が、酒を飲みに来ており、事件のおりに居合わせましたところ、手傷をおいました。一紀は逃げ去り、近所の者どもがあちこち尋ねましたが、ゆくえ知れずになりました。岩二郎と孫三郎はただちに大阪屋へ逃げ帰りました。このほかに、

明置き候へとも内へは外より遣入るところ無之候　然る処夜番のもの便所へ罷り越し候　うち其節遣入

候哉と奉レ存候　且又今暁牛谷と申すもの罷り越しレ一紀儀私レ方へ遣入り候　趣　承りはり及び候　由

に付可レ二相渡一旨申聞候　処、家来片岡政右衛門罷り出、長官へ申送り候　間暫く差控へ候　様申し聞

自害に及び候　も申し聞せす候　段は一紀を囲る候　様申し聞き全く政右衛門心得違ひの儀私　に於て

奉二恐れ入一候　右一紀立帰り候趣　にて町内騒動仕り候　はゞ早速起き出家来内取しまり等吟味可レ仕

のところ手後れに相成其上一紀自害仕　り居候はゞ早速家来付置諸事可レ二心附一のところ長官差図有之

候迄手延に致置き候　不行届き取斗ひ不調法の至り奉二恐入一候　尚又悴勘解由儀若レ輩の儀其他

の者どもは女の儀殊に間も隔レ候　儀に御座候　間何等の義とも一向相弁へ不申候　依て此段申上候

以上]

夜番の者が便所へいった間に一紀が忍びこんだというのはいいとして、牛谷なる役人と思われる者

が一紀がここに入ったそうだというと、家来が長官にきいてきますからしばらく待ってくれと待たせ

ておいて、いつの間にか侵入して自害していた、それをいわずに一紀を囲っていたかのごとくにいっ

たのは家来の心得ちがいだったというのは、いかにもいい訳がましい。　役人を待たせておいて、その

間に、一紀に擬装の自害をさせたととれる。

五日の日付で事件のあった油屋からも主人清右衛門の名で奉行所へ届出があった。　その中に「阿州

居合わせた客はございません。

Three people by the name of Itarō, Iwajirō, and Magosaburō, apparently merchants from Awa province, who were staying at the place of Ōsakaya Sakuemon, and were over to have sake, happened to be at the site, and were wounded. Ikki fled, and though neighbors searched various places, his whereabouts were unknown. Iwajirō and Magosaburō instantly ran back to Ōsakaya. Besides these three, there were no other guests.

登楼する to visit a pleasure house. 　　いくらなんでもおかしい it is odd no matter how one looks at it. 　　節句の宵宮 the small celebration that occurs on the eve of a festival. 　　当の一紀 Ikki, the man in question. 　　敵娼を「まわし」でよそへもっていかれていたくらいであった [the place was so crowded that Ikki] even had his companion for the evening taken away to wait on other guests.

50. 丘陵地帯の尾根 the ridge of the hilly area. 　　外宮と内宮 the Outer and Inner Shrines of Ise. 　　唯一の参道 the only path to the Shrine. 　　古市寒風 Kanpū in Furuichi, a place name. 　　倭町を経て現在「間の山」というと、ここを指す尾部坂なる急な長い坂を登って going through Yamato town and climbing a steep slope called Obe slope, which is what one refers to as "Ai no Yama" these days [that is, in the 20th century of the narrator's telling]. 　　浦田町より牛谷坂というこれも尾部坂よりも急な坂を登って from Urata, climbing up a slope called Ushitani Slope that was also steep, in fact steeper than the Obe slope. 　　どちらからどちらへの参宮も no matter which visiting path one took, from the Inner to the Outer Shrine or vice versa. 　　どちらの聖地からも、急な坂、しかも道の悪い坂を上りつめた高いところに悪所(あくしょ)があった travelling from either of the two sacred places (the Inner and Outer Shrines), at the end of a steep slope, and a treacherous slope at that, was that place of ill repute. 　　古市遊廓 the Furuichi pleasure quarters. 　　寛政六年の大火 the great fire of the sixth year of the Kansei era (1794). 　　口の芝居、奥の芝居 the Playhouse at the Entrance and the Inner Playhouse, examples of the names of theatres in the pleasure quarters. 　　軒を接し eves touching eves; standing side by side. 　　江戸の吉原、京の島原と肩を並べる最盛期 at its peak, competing shoulder to shoulder with the Yoshiwara of Edo and Shimabara of Kyōto. 　　いかにも嘘らしい strikes [one] as particularly false.

商人の由にて同町大阪屋作右衛門方に罷在候、伊太郎、岩次郎、孫三郎、右三人の者酒給べに罷越居合せ候処、手疵為負、一紀儀は逃去り、近所の者共、所々相尋ね候得共行衛相知不申候、岩次郎孫三郎儀直ちに大阪屋へ逃帰り申し候、右の外居合せ候、客人は無御座候、」というところがある。四日の夜、一紀が油屋に登楼した時、阿波の商人三人しか客がなかったというのはいくらなんでもおかしい。油屋は大楼であり、その日は節句の宵宮である。しかも、当の一紀は敵娼を「まわし」でよそへもっていかれていたくらいであった。

ところで当時長峯一帯が、「間の山」と呼ばれたのは、その丘陵地帯の尾根が外宮と内宮との間にあって、唯一の参道であったからである。油屋のあるあたりは、丘陵の最高所で、古市寒風という地名であった。外宮からは、倭町を経て現在「間の山」というと、ここを指す尾部坂よりも急な長い坂を登って古市に至る。また内宮の方からは浦田町より牛谷坂というこれも尾部坂なる急な坂を登ってここに至る。どちらからどちらへの参宮も、古市を通らねばならなかった。つまり、どちらの聖地からも、急な坂、しかも道の悪い坂を登りつめた高いところに悪所があった。古市遊廓は、寛政六年の大火のあと栄えて妓楼七十軒以上あり、また口の芝居、奥の芝居という芝居小屋があり、その他旅館、料理屋、商店が軒を接し、江戸の吉原、京の島原と肩を並べる最盛期であった。その遊廓の中でも大楼といわれた油屋で、節句の宵宮に客が三人というのはいかにも嘘らしい。しかし、油屋主人清右衛

客商売のこととて because this was a matter of the entertainment industry.　納得できぬこともない [that Seiemon, the proprieter of Aburaya refrained from submitting clients' names in his report] was not impossible to understand.　それに反して in contrast.　藤波家からの届けのアイマイさ（曖昧さ）the ambiguity of the report submitted by the Fujinami family.

51. 神領（しんりょう, じんりょう）(1) the domain of a shrine, intended to provide revenues for sacred events, rituals, and construction; (2) domain ruled by the gods.　室町時代 the period when the Ashikaga ruled, 1336-1573.　内宮の門前町としての宇治、外宮の門前町としての山田の自治体 the self-governing communities of Uji as a shrine town of the Inner Shrine and Yamada as the shrine town of the Outer Shrine.　時の権力者でもどうにもならなかった even the ruler of the times could do nothing.

52. *This paragraph explains the ranks of families serving the Ise Shrine: the Jingū families (two in Uji and four in Yamada), Sanbō families (several tens in each of these two shrine towns), elder families (over one hundred just in Uji), and officials without a title. These details are unfamiliar to today's Japanese readers.*　当時の御師の最高位である神宮家に属している [The official Fujinami, an Inner Shrine's Oshi,] belonged to the Jingū families, the highest of the Oshi offices in those days.　三方家 the Sanbō families [ranked just under the Jingū families]. The term comes from 三方, a raised tray of unstained wood with decorative holes made on three sides and used for offering gifts to the gods and at other ceremonial occasions.　自治体政治の実権を握っていた [the Sanbō families] held administrative power over these self-governing communities.　各町の年寄職を兼ねる年寄家 Elder families who also served as elders in each town.

53. 平師職を手代として使い、全国に檀家をふやすための活動をさせていた [Oshi families] used rankless officials as assistants, engaging them in activities intended to increase parishioners throughout the country.　檀家 parish households (parish membership was by clan units, not individuals); also the hometown parish to which a person belonged even after moving elsewhere.　一回の参宮で消滅せぬばかりか not only did [the relationship between an Oshi and a parishioner] not vanish after one visit to the Ise Shrine but.　一旦結んだ師檀の縁を切ってほかの御師に移ることはできなかった [a parishioner] was unable to cut off the Oshi-parishioner tie once formed, to move to another Oshi.　ナワバリ（縄張り）(*lit.*) roped-in area, i.e., territory.　株 stocks.　檀から納められる初穂 the first sheaves of rice of the year offered [to Oshi] by parishioners.　といっても実際は金納が多いから、その収入は相当なものとなる since in many cases they

門が届出に客人の名前をださないのは、客商売のこととて納得できぬこともない。それに反して、藤浪家からの届のアイマイさには別の配慮、別の意図がにおう。

五一　伊勢の地は昔から神領であり、神領政治が行われていた。それが室町時代からのちになって自治政治になり、内宮の門前町としての宇治、外宮の門前町としての山田の自治体は、時の権力者でもどうにもならなかった。ということは、そこは神域であった。奉行所がおかれても、神域はくずれなかった。

五二　藤浪神主は、内宮の御師職であり、当時の御師の最高位である神宮家に属している。神宮家は宇治に二軒、山田に四軒あり、その下の三方家が宇治と山田に数十軒ずつあり、この三方家が自治体政治の実権を握っていた。この下に各町の年寄職をかねる年寄家は山田だけで百軒以上あった。さらに平師職が年寄の下にあった。

五三　御師職の家では平師職を手代として使い、全国に壇家をふやすための活動をさせていた。御師と壇家の関係は一回の参宮で消滅せぬばかりか、いったん結んだ師壇の縁を切って他の御師に移ることはできなかった。ということは師職の間には全国の壇家のナワバリがあり、それは守られた。したがって、御師の職がもつナワバリは一種の株となり、財産ともなり、売買の可能性もでてきた。壇家を多くもつ師職の家では、壇家から納められる初穂、といっても実際は金納が多いから、その収入は相当

were actually monetary payments, despite the name [of "first rice sheaves"], the family income [of these Shintō officials] amounted to a fair size.

54. 一紀自害の届が長官の名前で出されなかったことも、うなずける it is understandable that the report on Ikki's suicide was not submitted in the Chōkan's name.　その権力をもってすれば with his power.　飛びこんできた殺人犯を「自害」させることぐらいはできたであろう he would have been able to manage such a [trite] thing as making the murderer who had burst in [for help] "commit suicide." 飛びこんでくる is associated with a bird flying to one's arms.　家来筋にあたる福間太夫の息子を奉行所役人の手に渡さなかっただけである all he did was fail to deliver into the hands of the magistrate's officer the son of Fukuma Taifu who was his subordinate.　～にあたる to correspond to ～.

55. 自害して果てたことになっている息子 his son who was made out to have committed suicide.　いくら神域内でも生きかえらせることはできない even in a sanctuary it was impossible to bring [his son] back to life.　京都留学の評判をとる医者、福間一紀 Fukuma Ikki, a doctor famed for having studied in Kyōto. 世間に出すこと to send [Ikki] out into society; make him successful.

56. 三日もすると in three short days.　快復していた had already recovered. 申し訳のひっかき疵 a mere excuse of a scratch.　もし検使役人の書くような、深さ一寸五分、長さ八寸余の疵で生きておれたら奇蹟だ (semi-indirect speech) it would be a miracle if I survived with such a wound as the examiner wrote about, one and a half inches deep and over eight inches long. The following two sentences use direct narration, Ikki talking to his father.　さむらいでもそんなに腹を切りはしませんよ even a samurai wouldn't slit his belly [that deeply]　八寸余りも切り裂いたら、内蔵が飛び出しますよ if one cut open as much as eight inches, the intestines would jump out.

57. 粥を炊く to cook rice gruel. Instead of regular rice, it was customary to serve gruel, which was easier for the sick to digest.　下男ひとりを残して keeping one male servant.　使用人はすべて暇を出してあった [Fukuma] had dismissed all his servants.　事の次第は一切外部へもらすな not to leak anything at all about how things had happened.　と伝えられてきていた word had been sent [from Fujima].

なものとなる。

五四　藤浪家の長官は、こういう御師職の最高の地位にある人物である。藤浪家からの一紀自害の届が長官の名前で出されなかったことも、うなずける。そしてまた、その権力をもってすれば飛びこんできた殺人犯を「自害」させることぐらいはできたであろう。長官は家来筋にあたる福間大夫の息子を奉行所役人の手に渡さなかっただけである。

五五　ところが、福間大夫は、助けられた息子をどうするのか。自害して果てたことになっている息子を、いくら神域内でも生きかえらせることはできない。京都留学の評判をとる医者、福間一紀をもう一度世間に出すことは不可能である。

五六　一紀は三日もすると快復していた。腹の疵は、申し訳のひっかき疵である。もし検使役人の書くような、深さ一寸五分、長さ八寸余の疵で生きておれたら奇蹟だと医者の一紀は笑う。さむらいでもそんなに腹を切りはしませんよ、八寸余りも切り裂いたら、内臓が飛び出しますよ、と一紀はいう。

一紀は笑う。

五七　父親は息子に、粥を炊き、湯を沸かした。息子の着ているものを洗った。藤浪長官から、事の次第は一切外部へもらすなと伝えられてきていた。

用人はすべて暇を出してあった。下男ひとりを残して、使た。

58. 思案 thought; reflection; rumination.　一紀が「殺された」無念をどうおさ
め、どう晴らせばいいのか [Fukuma wondered] how to pacify his vexation at Ikki
having "been killed," and revenge himself for it. As a Buddhist term, 無念 means
thoughtlessness free of mortal attachments, but here it is synonymous to 残念（ざん
ねん）. It is not common to use おさめる (to rule, subdue, put back, put away)
with 無念; 無念をはらす (to clear away one's vexation, i.e., to revenge oneself)
is a fixed phrase.　福間大夫の息、医師福間 一紀は殺されてしまった [though
Fujinami kindly saved Ikki's life,] Fukuma Ikki, Fukuma Taifu's son the doctor, had
been effectively killed [by the public sham suicide].

59. ころげるように降りた descended [the slope] as if to tumble down.　昔、罪
人の首斬りを忌みきらった神域が、罪人を突き落としたという地獄谷と呼ば
れるところだったのか Was that (the location to which Ikki descended) the place
called the Valley of Hell, into which the sanctuary, with its aversion to beheading
criminals, is said to have [the executioners] thrust criminals in the old days?　坂上
の闇に誘われるように登っていったのに despite the fact that he ascended as if
drawn to (or, enticed by) the darkness atop the slope.　そこからころげ落ちたと
ころも暗闇だった the place that he had fallen to was also dark.

60. 髪の伸びた一紀の顔 the face of Ikki whose hair had grown long.　蒼白い
というより白っぽい灰色に見える seemed ashy white rather than pale.　押し
つけて横たえる forced [Ikki] down in his bed.　盗み見る to take a stealthy
look.　ひとりごちる to talk to oneself.　媚びるような coquettish; fawning;
favor-currying. *That Fukuma earlier stole a glance at the beautiful face of Ikki and
that Ikki now casts a fawning eye at Fukuma once again characterizes the nature of
their relationship.*

五八

一紀をどうすればいいのか、と福間大夫は思いつづけていた。一紀が家に運びこまれた時からその思案はつづいていた。一紀が「殺された」無念をどうおさめ、どう晴らせばいいのか。藤浪長官は息子の命を救ってくれたが、一紀が「殺された」。福間大夫の息、医師福間一紀は殺されてしまった。

五九

「五日の日はどこへいった」と大夫は問うたが、一紀は答えぬ。

あの時、どの家の脇からころげるように降りたか一紀は覚えていない。昔、罪人の首斬りを忌みきらった神域が、罪人を突き落したという地獄谷と呼ばれるところだったのか。ただ、闇の中を歩いたことしか思い出せない。登っていった坂も、尾部坂だったか牛谷坂だったかさえ思い出せない。坂の上の闇に誘われるように登っていったのに、そこからころげ落ちたところも暗闇だった。そんな記憶しかない。

六〇

髪の伸びた一紀の顔は、蒼白いというより白っぽい灰色に見える。

「まだ起きぬ方がいい」と父親は起き上りかける息子を押しつけて横たえる。

美しい息子の顔を、大夫は盗み見る。

「松尾村では近すぎるか」大夫はひとりごちる。

「松尾村に？　あんなところへどうして」と息子は、媚びるような目を大夫に向ける。

そうだ、あの時、松尾村で弟に追いかえされた、と一紀は思い出す。

61. せっかく医者になったものを　when you finally made it as a doctor [it's a pity that your life is ruined]. ものを, a paradoxical conjunction, works like のに. 愚痴めいてきた put on an air of complaint.　檀家であった鳥羽 Toba, his parish.　少年の一紀を一目見たときの、たかぶったきもち a sense of excitement when [Fukuma] had his first glimpse of Ikki as a boy.

62. 身なりを見ればわかったろう [the maid] would have known from my outfit [that I had money].　五ツ紋の羽織 formal kimono jacket decorated/imprinted with the family crest, one each on the back, each sleeve, and each side of the chest. 一つ紋 and 三つ紋 are less formal alternatives.　大小は腰にあった I wore both swords at my [left] hip [thrust through my sash].

63. 無智（無知）な者どもが those ignorant people! The plural ども is derogatory. が works as an emotive particle with a meaning of invective.　きたない者どもが those filthy people!　そのきたないところへいったのは、他ならぬお前 (lit.) the one who went to that filthy place is none other than you; you are the one who went to that filthy place!　そのきたない者どもにお前が殺されて はたまらぬ I won't suffer you to be killed by those filthy people.　浮かんだ occurred [to Fukuma].

64. *This paragraph conveys the thought that occurred to Fukuma in the manner of semi-indirect speech.*　この家の外では死んだことになっている outside this house, [his son] was assumed dead.　なにも、一紀をここから逃す算段をすることはなかった there was no need at all to contrive a way to let Ikki escape from here.　ここにいる限りは as long as he stayed here.

「せっかく医者になったものを」と父親のひとり言は愚痴めいてきた。

大夫は少年の日の一紀を思い出している。壇家であった鳥羽のさむらいの家で少年の一紀をひと目見た時の、たかぶったきもちが昨日のことに思える。

「あの仲居は、わたしを見て金をもたぬと思ったのか。いやそうじゃない。身なりを見ればわかったろう。わたしはあの時、たしか五ツ紋の羽織を着て、大小は腰にあった。とにかくあの家へ入った時から、わたしは客の扱いを受けなかった」と一紀は目をつむったまま喋っていた。

「無智な者どもが」と一紀はいい、「きたない者どもが」といった。

「そのきたないところへいったのは、他ならぬお前。しかし、そのきたない者どもにお前が殺されてはたまらぬ」と大夫はいったが、ふいに、今まで思ってもみなかったことが浮んだ。

息子は死なずに生きている。その息子はこの家の外では死んだことになっている。ということは、息子は、生きるためにはこの家から外へは出てゆけぬ。外へ出ていくことは死ぬことである。とすれば、息子はずっとここにいることになる。医者福間一紀は死んだが息子はここから離れないということになる。息子は、もうあの急な坂を登ることはできないということである。なにも、一紀をここから逃がす算段をすることはなかった。世間での一紀はもう死んだのだ。ただ自分の息子は死なずにここにいる。ここにいる限りは生きつづける。

65. よろこびが液体のようにしみ出てくるのを that joy exuded [from the interior of his body] like liquid.　一紀に悟られまいと身構えていた [Fukuma] was on his guard so as not to let Ikki sense that. . . . *Fukuma is happy that Ikki will never again patronize women but will stay by his side. Although Ikki is already aware of Fukuma's sentiment, Fukuma himself is still guarding his secret.*　充分の養生をした上で after sufficient recuperation　すでに前から縁を切ってあったことにしていただいて I'll ask you to pretend that you had already cut off ties with me.　ゆるやかにうねるよろこびを抑えて suppressing the joy that slowly undulated inside him. *Note the expressiveness of the hiragana in comparison with* 緩やかにうねる喜び(悦び, 歓び, 欣び).

66. 首に縄かけてでもしばりつけておかないのですか why don't you keep me tied down even if it takes putting a rope around my neck?　無謀な reckless.　父上のいわれる通りにしますよ I will do as you say. 父上 is more formal and archaic than お父さん in modern Japanese, although it is sometimes still used in directly addressing one's father in letters. It is common, even today, to say 父上 or お父上 in referring to another's father.

67. 大根を切るようにひとを斬ったんですからね why, I slew human beings [as easily] as if slicing white radishes.　恐怖でゆがんだ人間の顔 a human face distorted with fear.　私が逆上した果ての人殺しとは思われないでしょう I'm sure you don't think it was murder [committed] as a result of my frenzy; you don't think I was at my wit's end when I killed those people.　殺人しといわれたから人殺しをしただけ I murdered them only because [they called me] a murderer. 息子を人殺しにするつもりで with an intention of making your son a murderer.

大夫は、自分のからだの内部からよろこびが液体のようにしみ出てくるのを、そばにいる一紀に悟

六五
られまいと身構えていた。

「とにかく充分の養生をした上で考えよう」と大夫はいった。

「いつまでもここに忍んでいる訳にもいきません。わたしとはすでに前から縁を切ってあったことに

していただいて、京都の方へでもいくかして――」と一紀は思いつめたようにいった。

「いや、当分はとにかく養生して――」と大夫は、ゆるやかにうねるよろこびを抑えて息子にいった。

六六
「わたしはもう死んでいるんですから、ここにいるのは死者なんですね。しかし、実際は、人殺しで

すよ。人殺しがここから出歩けば、どうなるでしょう。いちばん困るのは藤浪長官でしょうね。勿論、

福間大夫もです。わたしを、どうして外へ出ないように、首に縄かけてでもしばりつけておかないの

ですか。もう二、三日もすれば、わたしはどこにでも出歩ける。大阪ぐらいならゆけますよ。しかし

わたしはそんな無謀なことはしません。ここにいて、父上のいわれる通りにしますよ。もうわたしは

死んだのですから。

六七
わたしは、油屋で、大根を切るようにひとを斬ったんですからね。恐怖でゆがんだ人間の顔を見る

のは痛快だった。父上も、わたしが逆上した果ての人殺しとは思われないでしょう。わたしは、人殺

しといわれたから人殺しをしただけですから。

68. めったなことでは酔わない I don't get drunk easily; I rarely get drunk. めったな means rash, indiscreet, or, with a negative, rare.　理由なんぞありません I didn't have any such thing as a reason.　なんぞ is synonymous with なんど, なんか, and なんて.　女は、なにもあんなところへいかなくてもいる women, if that's what one wants, are available even if one doesn't go to such a place; it doesn't require a trip to that kind of place to meet a woman. なにも…… [negative form of verb] ても is emphatic.　田舎者の真似をして imitating rustics. *Ise Shrine visitors from distant rural areas were often ridiculed as bumpkins.*

69. 利発な bright.　ここにかくれているしかなくなりましたね there is nothing you can do but hide here [alone with me].

70. 思わず握りしめた squeezed [Ikki's hand] before thinking; a rather rare gesture for a father toward a grown son.

父上は、まさか息子を人殺しにするつもりで十五歳のわたしをここへつれてきたのではなかったでしょうに。

酒を下さい。もう酒を飲んでもかまわない。

あの時、酒に酔ってはおりませんでしたよ。医者のわたしがいうのだから。

のは父上もよくご存じでしょう。酔うほど飲んでいないし、めったなことでは酔わない

父上は。理由なんぞありませんね。女は、なにもあんなところへいかなくてもいる。なにも田舎者の

真似をしてあんなところへいかなくても。

わたしも、父上がしたように、もし年をとれば、あの時のわたしのような利発な少年を息子にしよ

うと思ってた。

これからずっと、父上は息子のわたしとふたりだけで、ここにかくれているしかなくなりましたね。

わたしは外へ出てゆけない。外では、わたしはすでに死んでいる。死者が外を歩けない。この家で

しかわたしは生きておれないということですね、安心なさったでしょう」と一紀は横たわったまま、

喋りつづけた。

「お前のいう通りだ」と大夫は一紀の手をとり、思わず握りしめた。

「お前は、あの時から少しも変っていない。利発で、美しい少年だったあの時から――」と大夫はいっ

藤浪長官のはからい（計らい）があっても even with Fujinami's intercession.
檀家を藤浪長官にゆだねるしか道はないだろう there would be no choice but
to place his parish families under Fujinami's disposal.

71. 医者一紀の看板をかかげてあてがった家 the house Fukuma had provided
for Ikki, with a signboard that said "Ikki, the Doctor."　　暇をやって追い払った
sent away [the only remaining manservant] by releasing him from his chores; discharged him to get rid of him.

72. 血色 complexion.　　水仕事 laundry and cooking.　　煮炊き (*lit.*) stewing
and boiling, i.e., cooking.　　白湯 plain hot water.　　井戸 well.　　汗ばんだ
slightly sweaty.　　ヘチマ loofah, a kind of summer squash (also called sponge
cucumber in English) that is used as a bath sponge.　　ひび割れて cracked.　　ザ
ラザラしている coarse, rough.

た。大夫の頭部の奥底には涙が湧いていたが外部へはこぼれなかった。

福間大夫は、もう自分自身についてはなにも考えていなかった。元のように、大夫としての師職をつづけられるかどうかも考えなかった。藤浪長官のはからいがあっても不可能だろう。壇家を藤浪長官にゆだねるしか道はないだろう。福間大夫も、福間一紀とともに消え去るのだと思った。

七一　同じ浦田町に、医者一紀の看板をかかげてあてがわれた家は売られることになるだろう。一紀はもう二度とあの家にいくことはない。

七二　ただひとり残していた下男にも暇をやって追い払った。もうここには大夫と一紀しかおらぬ。

七三　また二日たった。もう一紀が「自害」してから一週間目になる。

一紀の血色は良くなってきた。元通りだ、と大夫は思う。自分は元通りではない、と一紀は思う。二十七歳の男父親は下男の代りに水仕事をし、煮炊きもする。一紀は酒を飲む。父親は白湯を飲む。少年の日の一紀がした十七歳の息子の汗ばんだからだを拭く。父親が酒を運ぶ。父親が着物を洗う。父親の手の指、足の踵ように、井戸から水をくみ、父親のからだを洗うようなことはない。今は老いた父親が水をくみ、二五十歳をはるかに越えた男がそこにふたりでいる。ずっとふたりでいる。

は、乾いたヘチマのようにこまかくひび割れてザラザラしている。そのザラザラが、からだを拭いてもらっている一紀の皮膚に触れている。

73. 刀がすべるように落ちていきましたよ my sword [blade] went down as if to slide [through her flesh]; the sword slid down meeting no resistance. *Another instance of the main character's detachment from himself, with the sword as the performer of an action.*　　男を人間だなんて思ってやしない [women at that kind of place or anywhere else] hardly think that men are human beings. 思ってやしない is a colloquial form of 思っていはしない.

74. どうすれば少しでも、その人間じゃないものから遠ざかっておれるかを計っているんです I know she was measuring how she would be able to keep her distance, even if just a little, from that creature that was not a human being.　　その日のめし（飯）にありつくためじゃありません (*lit.*) it's not so as to barely get their day's food; they weren't doing it to scrape together a meal.　　人間じゃないものが、ため息ついて倒れるのを見とどける to witness the non-human creature collapse with a sigh.　　いったい、　なにがいいたいんだ、あいつらは what on earth do they [those women] want to say?

75. 一瞬一瞬が溶けていくように感じられる it felt [to Fukuma] as though each second dissolved into the next.　　なるべく息子を見つめぬようにしようと思うが though he tried as much as possible not to gaze at his son.　　自分の気持ちを察しているのが that [his son] understood his feelings.

「女を斬る時、刀が滑るように落ちていきましたよ。柔らかい肉の間を、刀が滑っていくのです。まるい肩から、まるい腕を滑っていくのですよ。斬るんじゃない、滑るんです。ああいうところの女は、いや、どこの女も、男を人間だなんて思ってやしない。その人間だなんて思ってやしない者がふいに刀になった。そうですよ、父上。

色の黒い、十四、五の子供みたいな女がきましたよ。その時、わたしは刀をもっていなかった。だからあの女は殺されなかった。あの色の黒い子供みたいな女だって、わたしを人間だと思ってやしない。小さな黒い目をしていた。その目で、どうすれば少しでも、その人間じゃないものから遠ざかっておれるかを計っているんです。その日のめしにありつくためじゃありません。人間じゃないものが、ため息ついて倒れるのを見とどけるのが女の商売です。笑いをこらえている。いったい、なにがいいたいんだ、あいつらは」と一紀は酒を飲みながら喋る。

大夫は息子の喋っていることを聴いてはいない。一瞬一瞬が溶けていくように感じられる。息子と過す時間が永遠につづくようにも、また次の瞬間に突然終わるようにも思われる。なるべく息子を見つめぬようにしようと思うが、そう思うと、かえって息子に目がゆく。大夫には、屋敷の外がいったいどうなっているかはどうでもいい。屋敷の外側にはもうなにもない。それに、なによりも、息子が、自分の気持を察しているのがうれしい。息子はここから出られないのを知っているといった。ここで

76. 山脇先生 Ikki's medical teacher at Kyōto. The name Yamawaki was chosen for the association with Yamawaki Tōyō (1705-1762), who conducted the first dissection in Japan, and his son Yamawaki Tōmon (1736-1782), who carried out several dissections.　からだがなまぬくい（生温い, also pronounced なまぬるい）熱をはらみ his body holding a tepid fever.　だるい幸福感 languid happiness.　オモリのごとくに沈殿してしまっている had settled like a weight.　寒気がするように落着かぬ he was restless as if he had the shivers.　恐怖がよろこびの触媒にもなり、また悪寒となる the fear [that everything might be over in the next moment] acted as a catalyst for joy but gave him a chill at the same time.

77. 落ち着きを失った restless.　一紀をつつみこむ（包み込む）ものではない [Fukuma's joy] was not of a nature that embraced Ikki.　なにかに憑かれたように、なにかを 振り払うように as though possessed by something, and as though brushing something away.　沈黙して端座していることはない [Fukuma] never sat straight in silence.

78. やっと、思い通りになりましたね finally things are as you have wished. *Here Ikki reveals his awareness of his father's feelings in more direct language than before.*　父上の思いのままです I am at your mercy.　わたしは生きたまま、父上に飼われていくんですね alive, I will be kept by you like a pet animal, will I not?

79. なんだ、こんなことがしたいのか [the woman's eyes say] I see, so this is what petty thing you want to do.

しか生きられないといった。安心してくれといった。

「京都の山脇先生のところで学んでいるころ——」と一紀は話しかけたが、「父上を悲しませるから、やめましょう」といった。

一紀がなにを話しても、大夫は聴いていない。からだがなまぬくい熱をはらみ、だるい幸福感が大夫の中にオモリのごとくに沈殿してしまっている。それなのに、寒気がするように落着かぬ。次の瞬間になにもかも終わるかもしれない、という恐怖がよろこびの触媒にもなり、また悪寒となる。

その落着きを失った福間大夫の動きが、一紀には不思議な景色にうつっている。大夫のよろこびは一紀をつつみこむものではない。普段、あれほどからだを動かすことのなかった人間が、なにかに憑かれたように、なにかを振り払うようにこまかく動きまわっている。沈黙して端座していることはない。

「やっと、思い通りになりましたね、父上。もうわたしはどこへもゆかないから。どこへもゆけない。父上の思いのままです。わたしは生きたまま、父上に飼われていくんですね。もう少しお酒を下さい。わたしは、あの油屋にいるような女と同じ目をしていませんか。いや、逆だ。父上がああいう目をしているんです。やっぱりそうじゃない。女の目は、なんだ、こんなことがしたいのか、父上が外に出てもいいのですから、買ってるんです。もう少し、お酒を。もうお酒はないのですか。

80. 闇の中へ into the dark; the evening dark as far as Fukuma is concerned, but the dark atop the slope is also implied.　　思いがかすかに（微かに，幽かに）横切る the thought faintly crossed [Fukuma's mind].　　毒だと知って飲む美味な液体がからだにしみこむようなよろこびにひたる (lit.) [Fukuma] was absorbed in a joy that resembled a sweet-tasting liquid, that one drank while knowing it to be poisonous, penetrating into the body; the joy that washed over [Fukuma] was like absorbing a sweet-tasting liquid that one drank knowing it to be poisonous.

81. 水桶を邸内に運び込んで bringing a wooden water bucket inside the house. 息たえて（絶えて）いた had breathed his last.　　はるかに深く far more deeply [than the examiners had recorded].　　咽喉のまん中に刀が突き立てられていた a sword was thrust into the center of his throat.

82. 宇治今北山墓地 the Imakitayama graveyard in Uji.　　正面に戒名 [Ikki's] postmortem Buddhist name [was carved] on the front of the grave stone.　　側面に俗名、および死んだときの年齢 his secular name and his age at death [carved] on one flank.　　寛政八丙辰年五月一四日 [and on another it says] "the 14th day of the fifth month of the eighth year of the Kansei era." The eighth year of Kansei (1789-1800) falls in 1796. 丙辰 (ひのえたつ, *alt.* へいしん), fire-older with dragon, is the 53rd of the 60-year cycle. This is a calendrical combination of the 3rd of the 10 stems and the 5th of the 12 branches. For a fuller explanation and a complete table of the sexagenary cycle, see under "jikkan jūnishi" in Kōdansha's *Japan: An Illustrated Encyclopedia.*　　後世ナゾとされてきた [the contradictory dates] have been held as a mystery in later days.

83. 今ひとつは the other [grave].　　大正末期 late in the Taishō era (1912-26). 実川延若 Jitsukawa Enjaku II (1877-1951), first born son of Enjaku I, was a famous Kabuki actor who was particularly skilled at *wagoto* (romantic stage).　　〜を模してつくってある is modeled after [the Imakitayama gravestone].　　坂東彦三郎 Bandō Hikosaburō IV (1800-73), who specialized in playing male leads.

きて下さい。これから長いんですからね。ずっとずっとこうしてふたりで喋っていなければならないんですから――」と一紀はいった。

〔八〇〕
夕闇のなか、福間大夫は庭へ出て、井戸から水をくんだ。夜がくるたびに、闇の中へ一紀が消えていきはせぬかという思いがかすかに横切る。そして一紀を見るたび、毒だと知って飲む美味な液体がからだにしみこむようなよろこびにひたる。一週間、それをくり返してきた。

〔八一〕
福間大夫が、水桶を邸内に運びこんで、一紀を座敷に見にいった時、すでに一紀は自害して息たえていた。藤浪家で検使役人が書いたたよりよりも、はるかに深く咽喉のまん中に刀が突き立てられていた。

〔八二〕
福間一紀の墓は二ツある。

ひとつは、というよりそれが一紀の墓なのであるが、宇治今北山墓地にある。正面に戒名、側面に俗名、及び死んだ時の年齢、二十七歳とあり、もう一方の側面に、寛政八丙辰年五月十四日とある。藤浪神主邸で「自害」したとある検使書は五月七日だった。七日と十四日のちがいが、後世ナゾとされてきた。

〔八三〕
今ひとつは、油屋のすぐ近所にある、古市大林寺に、おこんの墓と並んでつくられたものがある。これは、大正末期、歌舞伎役者の実川延若が建てたもので、宇治今北山墓地の墓碑を模してつくってある。おこんの墓は、江戸の歌舞伎役者坂東彦三郎の建立である。その坂東彦三郎は、事件から三十

文政一二年　the twelfth year of the Bunsei era (1818-29), or 1829.　　「奥の芝居」 the Inner Theater, the name of a playhouse.　　油屋の事件をネタにしてつくられた written based on the incident at Aburaya. ネタ is a cryptology made reversing the syllables of 種 (たね), seed, source, material.　　「切宝年菜種実」　the title of the kabuki play, roughly meaning "the last treasury harvest of rapeseeds." 切 puns on 切 (きり), the last scene of a play, and 斬る, to slay. 宝年 puns on 宝, treasure, and 豊年, rich harvest. 菜種実, oil-producing rapeseeds, alludes to the name of the pleasure house 油屋, Oil House.　　上演する to put on the stage.　　評判をとる to gain a reputation.　　その興行の成功のゆえに because of the success of the production.　　主人公おこんを供養して in commemoration of Okon, the protagonist.　　安政五年 the fifth year of Ansei (1854-59), or 1858, the year the US-Japan friendship and trade treaty was signed.　　「奥の芝居」にかかった時は when [the play] was performed at the Inner Theater.　　「伊勢音頭恋寝刃」 the title of the play, "Ise Song: Love's Dull Blade."　A play in 4 acts and 7 scenes written by Chikamatsu Tokuzō (1751-1810) and first produced in Ōsaka in 1796.　　外題 title of a play; originally a title written on a rectangular piece of paper pasted on the outside of a scroll.　　紛失した名刀と鑑定書を主筋のために探す目的で with the purpose of finding, for his master, the lost fine sword and its appraisal document. およそ事件とはかけはなれた(掛け離れた、懸け離れた)筋の芝居 a play with a plot line that was greatly removed from the incident.

84. 昭和の戦争の火 refers to the World War II firebombings.　　文政十二年己丑 1829, the last year of Bunsei. 己丑 (つちのとうし, *alt.* きちゅう), earth-younger with ox, is the 26th of the 60-year cycle.　　墓碑 grave stone inscription.　　長嶺 Nagamine, a place name in Ise; see 1 and 50 above.　　そばや (蕎麦屋)の娘 daughter of the owner of a soba-noodle shop.

三年後の文政十二年に古市中之地蔵町（古市寒風のとなり町）の「奥の芝居」で、油屋の事件をネタにしてつくられた、「切宝年菜種実」を上演して評判をとり、その興行の成功のゆえに主人公おこんを供養して墓をつくったのである。「切宝年菜種実」は安政五年に同じ中之地蔵「奥の芝居」にかかった時は「伊勢音頭恋寝刃」という外題になっていた。これは主人公が紛失した名刀と鑑定書を主筋のためにさがす目的で油屋へ入りこむという、およそ事件とはかけはなれた筋の芝居であった。

現在、油屋の建物はなんにも残っていない。寛政六年の大火のあと古市遊廓が生れ、その後全盛をきわめたが、すべては昭和の戦争の火で消え去った。尚、おこんは文政十二年己丑二月九日に、四十九歳で死んだのは墓碑によってわかるが、出身地も本名もわからない。長峯のそばやの娘だったという説もあるらしいが、確実なものはなにもない。

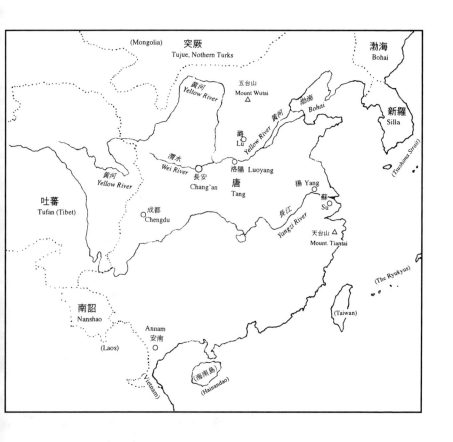

(Mongolia) 突厥 Tujue, Nothern Turks 渤海 Bohai

黃河 Yellow River 五台山 Mount Wutai 渤海 Bohai 新羅 Silla

潞 Lu

渭水 Wei River 黃河 Yellow River (Tsushima Strait)

黃河 Yellow River 長安 Chang'an 洛陽 Luoyang 揚 Yang

吐蕃 Tufan (Tibet) 唐 Tang 蘇 Su

成都 Chengdu 長江 Yangzi River 天台山 Mount. Tiantai

(The Ryukyus)

南詔 Nanshao (Taiwan)

Annam 安南 (Laos)

(Vietnam) (海南島) (Hainandao)

僧行賀の涙

井上 靖

The Tears of Priest Gyōga

Inoue Yasushi

INOUE YASUSHI (1907-91) was born in Ashikawa, Hokkaidō, where his father, an army medical officer, was stationed, but spent his elementary school days living with his grandmother in Yugashima on the Izu Peinsula. He began composing poems while at Numazu Middle School. He studied science at high school thinking of following his father's footsteps, but switched to humanities in college. After withdrawing from Kyūshū University, he enrolled at Kyōto University, where he devoted most of his time to literary activities. He graduated at the age of 29 with a degree in art history. By then he had had a play performed at Shinbashi Theatre, and had won a prize for a full-length novel.

In 1936, Inoue stopped writing fiction and joined the Ōsaka Mainichi newspaper. Drafted, he was sent to north China in 1937 but returned after seven months due to illness. Around 1940 he began associating with Ōsaka poets and resumed writing poetry.

In 1947 when he was forty, he again turned to writing fiction, and in 1951, he left the Ōsaka Mainichi to concentrate on writing. He produced a wide range of works, including fiction on contemporary social and political themes, popular love novels, autobiographical accounts, and historical narratives set in Japan and other Asian countries.

Tōgyū (1949, The Bullfight) and *Ryōjū* (1949, tr. *The Hunting Gun*), novellas published in the same year in the *Bungakukai*, were both well received. The former, which won the Akutagawa prize, concerns a managing editor of a new Ōsaka newspaper who is promoting a bullfight whose success will be crucial to the fate of his firm. *Kuroi ushio* (1950, The Black Tide) handles the Shimoyama incident (1949), in which the President of the National Railways was mysteriously killed. *Hyōheki* (1956-57, Wall of Ice), published serially in the *Asahi*, was inspired by a rope-climbing accident. It portrays two mountain climbers and a married woman they both admire. *Tōi umi* (1963, Distant Sea) was written for NHK's morning radio recitation program.

Shirobanba (1962, Dayflies), a portrayal, in the form of fiction, of Inoue's boyhood in Izu, and *Waga haha no ki* (1975, tr. Chronicle of My Mother), a memoir, represent his autobiographical writings.

Go-Shirakawa In (Retired Emperor Go-Shirakawa, 1972) is a portrait of the twelfth-century monarch based on diaries kept by attendants. In *Fūrinkazan* (1953-54, Wind, Forest, Fire, Mountain: an Account of Takeda

Shingen), *Sanada gunki* (1955, A Military Record of the Sanada), *Yodo-dono nikki* (1955-60, Diary of Lady Yodo), and many other novels and sto-ries, Inoue found his themes in the Sengoku period of the late sixteenth cen-tury.

Most importantly, Inoue Yasushi wrote a number of historical novels set in other parts of Asia including central Asia. *Tempyō no Iraka* (1957; tr. *The Roof Tile of Tempyō*, 1975) centers around the Chinese priest Ganjin (Jianzhen in Chinese), who, after five unsuccessful attempts, reached Japan in 754, at age 66 and blind, and the Japanese monks who sought to bring him to Japan as a proponent of Ritsu sect Buddhism. This proved to be one of the most memorable achievements of the Kentōshi system (Embassies to Tang China), under which the Japanese court sent at least 19 official mis-sions between 630 and 838. *Fūtō* (1963; tr. *Wind and Waves*) is an account of the Mongol invasions from the Korean perspective. Among other works of this genre are "Rōran" (1959; tr. "Loulan"), *Tonkō* (Dunhuang, 1959), *Saiiki monogatari* (1968-69; *tr. Journey beyond Samarkand*) and *Kōshi* (1987-89, Confucius). Rōran (Loulan in Chinese; original name Kroraina) was a small kingdom in central Asia, and Tonkō, a city in northwestern China, once prospered as a major center of trade on the Silk Road.

"Sō Gyōga no namida" (1954, The Tears of Priest Gyōga) portrays the life of an eighth century scholar monk who went to China on the 733 mis-sion and returned seven years after Priest Ganjin's voyage to Japan. Like Inoue's other historical narratives, this piece is characterized by control and precision, and respect for historical facts and details, all while telling a riv-eting story.

WORKS IN ENGLISH TRANSLATION

The Hunting Gun. Sadamichi Yako and Sanford Goldstein, trs. Tuttle, 1961.
The Counterfeiter, and Other Stories. Leon Picon, tr. Tuttle, 1965.
Chronicle of My Mother (Waga haha no ki). Jean Oda Moy, tr. Kodansha International, 1982.
Wind and Waves: a Novel (Fūrō). James T. Araki, tr. University of Hawaii Press, 1989.
Lou-lan and Other Stories (Rōran). James Araki and Edward Seidensticker, trs. Kodansha International, 1979.

1. **遣唐使** envoys to Tang China. The dispatch of envoys to the Tang began in 630, not long before the Nara period (710-794) and, after eighteen voyages, was discontinued in 894 in the Heian period (794-1192). In this story, Inoue Yasushi counts the 717 mission as the eighth, the 733 mission the ninth, and the 752 mission the tenth. With the historically overlooked 665 mission added as the fifth, the 717 mission is now known as the ninth, the 733 mission as the tenth, and the 752 mission as the eleventh.　**～の一団に加わって** joining the group of ～.　**留学僧** monk studying abroad.　**派遣する** to dispatch.　**孝謙天皇** Kōken Tennō (718-770), *r.* 749-758 and again 764-77 as Shōtoku Tennō (称徳天皇). She was the second daughter of Shōmu (聖武天皇) and Kōmyō Kōgō (光明皇后).　She abdicated in 758 in favor of Jun'nin (淳仁天皇), who was supported by her powerful cousin Fujiwara no Nakamaro. After Nakamaro's failed coup that ended in his death, she reascended the throne.　**天平勝宝** the second era (749-757) during Kōken's reign. The order was given in the second year in 750, but the actual departure occurred in 752. Of the four boats that comprised the mission, the first was destroyed on its way back from the Tang, while the second returned in 753 and the third and fourth in 754. **時に** at that time; often favored in historical narratives over その時.

2. **大和国広瀬郡** Hirose county in Yamato province.　**出家する** to renounce the world, enter the priesthood.　**興福寺** (*alt.* Kōbukuji) the head temple of Hossō Sect Buddhism and one of Nara's seven largest temples.　**永厳** the name of a priest at Kōfukuji.　**元興寺** (1) the original Gangōji, which was Japan's oldest temple, in Asuka in Nara prefecture; (2) also known as Shin-Gangōji (新元興寺), a Kegon Sect temple built in 718, one of Nara's seven largest temples. It played a part in many important state ceremonies during the Nara and Heian periods.　**平備** the name of a priest at Gangōji.　**その向学の心を認められて** his [Gyōga's] love of learning being recognized [by the government].　**勅命に依って** at imperial order.　**入唐**(にっとう、にゅうとう)**する** to enter Tang China.　**天台およ び法相の両宗義を修める** to master both Tendai and Hossō doctrines. Tendai (*Ch.* Tiantai), a sect based in Mt. Tiantai in Zhejiang province, was propagated in Japan by Priest Jianzhen (鑒眞, also written 鑑真, see 28) in the Nara period. The Hossō (*Ch.* Faxiang), transplanted from China by Genbō (see 6) and other priests, was located at Kōfukuji and Yakushiji, as well as some 55 other temples.

3. **遣唐大使** ambassador to Tang China. An embassy to Tang China was headed by officials of four ranks: 大使 (ambassador); 副使 (vice ambassador); 判官 (じょう、ほうがん); and 主典 (さかん) or 録事 (ろくじ). 判官, also written 尉 (じょう), was a general term for the third rank administrative offices in the four-level Ritsuryō system, and 主典, also written 佐官 or called 録事, that for the fourth-level administrative offices.　**藤原清河** dates unknown. Nara courtier and fourth son of Fujiwara no Fusasaki (681-737). He was sent to the Tang as ambassador in 752. On his way home the following year, his boat drifted to Annam

僧行賀の涙

一　僧行賀が第十回目の遣唐使の一団に加わって、留学僧として唐へ派遣されることになったのは、孝謙天皇の天平勝宝二年の九月である。時に行賀は二十二歳であった。

二　行賀は大和国広瀬郡の生まれで、十五の時出家し、興福寺の永厳および元興寺の平備について学んだが、その向学の心を認められて、勅命に依って、入唐することになったのである。天台および法相の両宗義を修めることが彼の留学の目的であった。

三　遣唐大使は藤原清河、副使は大伴古麿と決まり、判官、主典各四人の名前も発表された。こんどの遣唐使の一団は、唐の文化文物を輸入する目的のほかに、当時造営中であった東大寺の大仏に塗る

(present-day Vietnam). Narrowly escaping death, he returned to China and served the Tang court.　　副使 vice ambassador.　　大伴古麿 (?-757). Nara government official. Sent to China in 732 and again in 752, this time as vice ambassador. He brought home Priest Jianzhen, whose previous attempts to sail to Japan had failed. Komaro was put to death for having supported Tachibana no Naramaro's conspiracy. 判官、主典各四人 four each of third- and fourth- rank officials.　　文化文物 culture and cultural objects.　　当時造営中であった 東大寺の大仏に塗る金が 不足しているので since there was insufficient gold for painting Tōdaiji's great Buddha, which was under construction at that time.　　それを唐に求める使命を も併せ持っていた carried the added mission of acquiring it [the gold] in China.

4. どういうものか直ぐには実現を見ず [the mission] not for some reason materializing right away.　　翌三年 the following year, the third year of Tenpyō Shōhō. 渡唐 travelling to Tang China.　　吉備真備 (695-775). Nara period aristocrat and scholar. Sent in 717 to study in China where he stayed for 17 years and gained a degree of literary fame. He went to Tang China again in 752, returning in 764 to supervise the construction of Tōdaiji. He rose to the Minister of the Right (766) and Senior Second Order (769), but retired from the political scene following the death of Shōtoku (称徳).　　一切の準備なって (more colloquially 一切の準備がとと のって) all preparations having been completed.　　参朝する to present oneself to the imperial court.　　節刀を賜わる to be granted a sword. A ceremonial sword was bestowed on an envoy or expedition general dispatched at imperial order.　　無事大 任を果たして帰朝した折返進するものである one was expected to return it [the sword] when returning to Japan after safely carrying out the great task.　　順風を得 れば即時出発 immediate departure if favored by good wind.　　一日の逡巡も許 されないぎりぎりの立場に立つこと being in a no-retreat position that allowed not one day's hesitation.　　人選 selection of suitable persons.　　〜に費す to spend [time, money, etc.] on 〜.

5. この前の第九回の遣唐使 the previous mission, which was the ninth (733). 聖武天皇 45th sovereign; r. 724-749; ardent Buddhist remembered for the construction of the great Buddha statue of Tōdaiji; the era under Shōmu was marked by a flourishing of the arts under strong Chinese influence.　　天平五年 733 in Shōmu's reign.　　多治比広成 (?-739). Sailed to Tang China in 733, drifted to Tanegashima on the way back in 734, and returned to Nara in 735.　　中臣名代 (?-745). Sailed to Tang China with Tajihi no Hironari　　往路 the way out.　　帰路 the way back.　　惨憺たる miserable; disastrous.　　四隻の船に分乗して dividing up for separate rides on four boats.　　蘇州 Suzhou, a city in the southeast of China's Jiangsu province.　　洋上に消息を絶ち breaking off news at sea.　　崑崙 国 an old Chinese term referring to South Sea areas including present day Vietnam, Cambodia, and Malaysia.　　安南 Annam, an old term for present day Vietnam.　　乗 組員 crew.　　百十余人 over 110 people.　　土民 indigenous people; aborigines.

金が不足しているので、それを唐に求める使命をも併せ持っていた。

四　遣唐使派遣のことは発表されたが、どういうものか直ぐには実現を見ず、一年を経過した翌三年の秋に、渡唐の経験のある吉備真備が、大伴古麻呂のほかに更に副使として加わることが発表され、一切の準備なって、大使、副使が参朝し、節刀を賜わったのは翌四年三月のことである。節刀は無事大任を果たして帰朝した折返進するものであるが、これを賜わるということは、順風を得れば即時出発という一日の逡巡も許されないぎりぎりの立場に立つことを意味していた。人選の発表になってから節刀を賜わるまでに一年半以上の期間が、渡唐の準備のために費されたのである。

五　遣唐使の派遣は二十年目のことであった。この前の第九回の遣唐使は聖武天皇の天平五年で、多治比広成が大使、中臣名代が副使となって五百九十四名が渡唐した。この天平五年の場合は往路は無事だったが、帰路は惨憺たるものであった。一行は四隻の船に分乗して天平六年十一月蘇州を発ったが、そのうち無事だったのは二隻だけで、一隻は洋上に消息を絶ち、残りの一隻は遠く崑崙国（安南南部）に吹き流され、その乗組員百十余人は土民に襲われたり、病歿したりして、僅かに四名が再び唐土に舞い戻るという結果になった。そしてその生存者たちはこんどは船便を得て渤海路を取って帰国しようとしたが、この時もまた難船の憂目を見、着のみ着のまま天平十一年に出羽に漂着するという有様であった。

~に襲われる to be visited or assaulted by ~.　　病没する to die of illness.
舞い戻る to drift back.　　生存者 survivors.　　船便を得る to find an available
boat.　　渤海路 the Bohai route. Bohai (*Korean* Parhae) is a kingdom that ruled the
area from the southeast of Northeast China to the southern Korean peninsula from
698-926, and was known by that name starting in 713.　　難船の憂き目を見る to
suffer the misery of a shipwreck.　　着のみ着のままで with nothing but the
clothes one happens to be in.　　天平十一年 the year 739.　　出羽 Dewa province,
the present Yamagata prefecture.　　有様 plight.

6. 併し（然し）however.　　故国 one's native land/country.　　~に依って by
means of.　　在唐十九年の who lived in Tang China for 19 years.　　僧玄昉
Priest Genbō (?-746). He studied the doctrines of the Hossō sect in Tang China.
唐僧道璿 Chinese priest Dōsen (*Ch*. Daoxuan, 702-760), also known as 道叡 (ど
うえい). He came to Japan in 736, 18 years prior to the arrival of Ganjin, and
transmitted the precepts and teachings of the Kegon Sect. Kibi no Makibi left a
biography of Dōsen.　　印度婆羅門僧僊那 Bramin priest Bodhisena (*J*. Bodai-
senna, 704-760) from India. He visited Ganjin at Tōdaiji in 754.　　林邑国の僧仏哲
the monk Fozhe (dates of birth and death unknown) from Champa (now part of
Vietnam). In Japan he taught Buddhist dances as court music instructor.　　異国
foreign country.

7. 経史 a collective term for the basic Chinese classics and histories.　　陰陽暦算
yin and yang philosophy and calendrical math.　　百般に通じる to become thoroughly familiar (with).　　経論 sutras and commentaries. 経 (preachings of the
Buddha) and 論 (compilations of annotations on the sutras) are two categories of
三蔵 (さんぞう), or the Three Treasures of Buddhism, along with 律 (りつ) (religious precepts).　　奥義 the heart (of teachings); secret principles

8. 生命がけの仕事 a task performed at the risk of one's life; life-threatening task.
試みる to attempt.　　元正天皇 (680-748, r.715-724). Daughter of Genmei (元明
天皇), daughter of Tenji. Genshō contributed to the compilation of the Yōrō
Ritsuryō.　　養老元年 717, the first year of the Yōrō era (717-724).　　第八回のそ
れ the eighth embassy (by the author's count as discussed in no.1).

9. 青年僧 a youthful monk.　　知乗船事 Kentōshi officer, below the principal
four ranks, who handled matters related to the boat and shipping.　　都匠 officer
responsible for water conservancy.　　訳語 (おさ) interpreter. Cf. *mod. J* 訳語 (や
くご), terms used in translation.　　占人 diviner.　　陰陽師 (おんようじ, おん
みょうじ) diviner; astrologer.　　画師 painter.　　必要人員 required staff.　　学
問僧 scholar monk.　　~を混じえて including ~.

10. 珍しく unusually; uncommonly.　　天候に恵まれ favored or blessed with

併し、無事に故国に着いた二船に依って、在唐十九年の留学生の吉備真備、僧玄昉は帰り、唐僧道

璿や印度婆羅門僧僊那、林邑国の僧仏哲等の異国の僧たちが日本の土を踏んだのであった。

吉備真備は経史を研究し、陰陽暦算を初め、唐文化百般に通じて帰り、僧玄昉の方は経論五千余巻

と多くの仏像を故国に持ち帰った。真備に依って新しい教育が、玄昉に依って法相の奥義が伝えられ

たのである。

六、

　遣唐使派遣の成果は大きかったが、その犠牲も大きく、派遣される方にしてみると、全くの生命が

けの仕事であったので、遣唐使派遣はこれを屢々試みるというわけには行かなかったのである。この

第九回の遣唐使派遣と、その前の元正天皇の養老元年の第八回のそれとの間にも、やはり十数年の歳

月が置かれている。

八、

　青年僧行賀が加わった第十回遣唐使の一団は、大使、副使、判官、主典のほかに、随員として、知

乗船事、都匠、医師、占人、陰陽士、訳語、画師等の必要人員が加わり、それに学問僧、留学生を混

じえて五百名近い人数となり、それが四隻の船に分乗したのである。行賀は副使吉備真備の乗る第二

船に配された。

七、

　この航海は珍しく天候に恵まれ、四隻とも無事に、一カ月の後に、揚子江口に到着したが、行賀は

吉備真備と同船したために、航海中、彼の身辺にあって、親しくこの日頃尊敬している在唐研鑽の経

weather.　楊子江口 the mouth of the Yangzi River.　彼の身辺にあって、親し
く日頃尊敬している在唐研鑽の経歴を持つ知識人の風貌に接することが出
来た he [Gyōga] was able to stay near him [Kibi no Makibi] and enjoy intimate
contact with this intellectual whom he had always respected, a man with a record of
rigorous study in Tang China. 風貌に接する means "to come into personal contact"; 風貌 by itself means "appearance."

11. 彼を除く総ての者 all except him [Kibi no Makibi].　一片の雲にも、一滴
の雨にも、一喜一憂した alternated between hope and despair because of a mere
fragment of cloud or drop of rain.

〜を意に介する to worry about, mind.　顔は皺で刻まれ his [Makibi's] face
was deeply carved with wrinkles.　黒い斑点が無数に滲み出していた numerous dark freckles had surfaced [on the skin of his limbs].　彼がその身につけて
いる雰囲気 the atmosphere he cloaked himself in.　帆柱 mast.　端坐して
seated upright in a proper manner.　横になって午睡をとる to take a nap in a
reclining position.　船暈い（船酔い）と難破に対する恐怖でぐったりと死んだ
ようになっている人々の横たわっている船内 inside the boat, where people lay
limply as though dead from seasickness and fear of shipwreck.　気難しい hard to
please.

12. 養老元年の渡唐とこの前の第九回遣唐船での帰国と the 717 voyage to
Tang China and the return voyage to Japan aboard one of the boats of the previous
embassy, which was the ninth (by the author's count, as discussed in no. 1).　彼の
持っている落ち着きは、そのため許りではないと思われた the composure he
had did not seem to be only because of that [his travel experience].　永年経史を
修め衆芸を極めた人にして初めて持ちうる落ち着き composure attainable
only by one who has long studied Chinese classics and mastered a variety of arts.
〜した人にして (or であって) 初めて〜しうる is a fixed phrase, meaning "one
who has done 〜 alone can do 〜."

13. 吉備真備の将来した唐の書籍 Chinese books that Kibi no Makibi brought
back.　唐礼 Tang Li, the Tang version of Zhou Li (周礼, J. Shurai with a short u),
Rituals of Zhou, a reconstruction in the Confucian tradition of the governmental
structure of Zhou times.　大衍暦経、大衍暦立成 the *jing* (経, authentic text) and
licheng (立成, or lichengfa 立成法, astronomical calculation method) portions of
the Tang calendar Dayanli (大衍暦) in 18 parts, prepared by Priest Yixing (一行; J.
Ichigyō) at the order of Emperor Xuanzong. Starting in 729 it was used for 33 years
in China, and in Japan for 94 years from 764.　楽書要録 Essentials of 楽書
(*Book of Music*, Ch. Yueshu).　いずれにせよ in any case; either way.　彼など
の想像もつかぬ未知の厖大な知識の集積 immense accumulation of unknown
knowledge that the likes of him [Gyōga] could not even begin to imagine.

歴を持つ知識人の風貌に接することが出来た。

彼を除く総ての者は、一片の雲にも、一滴の雨にも一喜一憂したが、吉備真備だけは全然天候というものを意に介していなかった。彼はその時、六十歳近く、顔は深く皺で刻まれ、手足の皮膚には黒い斑点が無数に滲み出していたが、彼がその身につけている雰囲気は驚くほど若々しかった。帆柱の下の部屋を覗くと、大抵の時に端坐して読書しており、時には横になって午睡を取っていることもあった。朝と晩だけ、彼はそこを出て、船暈いと難破に対する恐怖でぐったりと死んだようになっている人々の横たわっている船内をゆっくりと歩いた。誰にも言葉はかけなかったが、決して気難しくはなかった。

二行賀には吉備真備だけが一行の中で別人に見えた。真備は養老元年の渡唐と、この前の第九回遣唐船での帰国と、併せて二回の航海の経験を持っており、こんどの航海は三度目のわけであったが、併し、彼の持っている落着きは、そのため許りではないと思われた。永年経史を修め衆芸を究めた人にして初めて持ち得る落着きであろうか。

二行賀は曾て吉備真備の将来した唐の書籍を見たことがある。行賀十五歳の時のことである。『唐礼』百三十巻、『大衍暦経』一巻、『大衍暦立成』十二巻、『楽書要録』十巻等々、それらはいかなる分野の書物か見当はつかなかったが、いずれにせよ、彼などの想像もつかぬ未知の厖大な知識の集積

正視できぬようなきらきらしたもの [giving off] a glitter that made it hard to gaze at them directly, [the books lay quietly, piled up on the corridor floor].

14. 心外 unexpected (in a negative way); annoying; offensive.

15. わたしはまた、君が怖がっているのかと思った I suspected that you were afraid. また is a light expression meaning "by chance, possibly, if at all."　何となく怯えが目の光の中にあるように思われる (*lit.*) somehow it seems to me fear is in the light of your eyes; i.e., I thought I saw a hint of fear in your eyes.　雨雲も、わしの乗っているこの船は避けて行く（よけていく／さけていく）rain clouds, too, circumvent this boat that I am on, if not other boats.

16. それはたいして応えなかった [being told that there was fear in his eyes was objectionable, but] did not hit him very hard. *The real reason for his surprise appears four sentences later on the next page.*　年の割にひどく老けていた he [Gyōga] looked quite old for his age.　背の低いうえに猫背でもあり he was not only short but stooped.　書物を目の前へ持っていかないと、文字が判読できなくなっていた unless he brought a book right up to his eyes, he no longer could make out what was written.

であることだけは明らかであった。正視できぬようなきらきらしたものを持ちながら、それらが静か

に興福寺の廻廊の床の上に重ねて置かれてあったのを行賀は印象深く覚えている。

航海中、行賀は一度だけ、真備から言葉をかけられたことがあった。

「怖いかな」

そう言う言葉であった。

「怖くはありません」

行賀は怖いかと聞かれたことが心外だった。

「それなら、宜しい。わたしはまた、君が怖がっているのかと思った。いつ見ても書物を読んでいる

ことは感心だが、それから眼を離す時、何となく怯えが眼の光の中にあるように思われる。船など怖

いものではない。わしなど三回目だが、いつでも航海は無事平穏だ。雨雲も、わしの乗っているこの

船は避けて行く」

行賀は驚いて伏せていた顔を上げた。自分の眼に怯えがあるといわれたことは不服だったが、それ

はたいして応えなかった。行賀は年の割にひどく老けていた。背の低い上に猫背でもあり、彼は自分

の姿も、表情も、自分を見る者に快い印象を与えないことを幼時から知っていた。それにここ数年

の烈しい読書のために眼を悪くしており、書物を眼の前へ持って行かないと、文字が判読出来なくなっ

そうした行賀の全体の印象と、対象を伺い見るようにする独特の視線の据え方から [Makibi might have thought Gyōga cowardly] from his overall impression and from his peculiar way of fixing his gaze that made it seem as though he were peering/spying at an object.　それはよかった That was acceptable. [However, he did not understand where Makibi's confidence came from.]　その自信の拠って来るところは、全然見当がつかなかった He had no idea whatsoever as to where that confidence came from. 拠って来るところ is a fixed phrase meaning "source"; 来る (きたる), slightly archaic, roughly corresponds to *mod. J.* 来ている.

17. ふと自分の傍で小さい笑い声の洩れるのを耳にした Gyōga chanced to hear a little burst of laughter from somewhere close at hand.　仙雲 the name of another scholar monk on the boat.　玄昉の門 disciple of Priest Genbō.　秀才 talented man, bright student.

18. そうしていることに依って by keeping that posture (lying supine with his mouth open).　蒼い顔の中で髯の延びたのが目立ち、時々開いている口から大きい吐息が洩れるのが聞こえた The unshaven whiskers stood out on his pale face, and from time to time a large sigh escaped from his open mouth.

19. そんな弱り方はしていたが、眼だけは行賀と違って不遜だった despite his weakened state, unlike Gyōga he [Sen'un] had something arrogant in his eyes–if only in his eyes.　じろりと相手をねめつける（睨め付ける）ように見た Sen'un looked at Gyōga as if to glare at him.

ていた。真備は、そうした行賀の全体の印象と、対象を窺い見るようにする独特の視線の据え方から、彼を臆病と思ったのかも知れなかった。それはよかった。併し、行賀は真備の雨雲が自分を避けて行くという自信が、どこから来るものであるか判らなかった。その自信の拠って来るところは、全然見当がつかなかった。

一七　真備はそれだけ言うと、行賀の傍を離れて行ったが、その時、行賀は、ふと自分の傍で小さい笑い声の洩れるのを耳にした。笑ったのは、この船に乗ってから初めて口をきき出した彼と同じ留学僧の仙雲だった。仙雲は玄昉の門で、行賀より年齢は三つ上だった。大きい顔と、手と、体とを持っていて、その名前は何回か耳にしたことがあったが、会ったのはこの船に乗ってからが初めてであった。

彼は秀才として知られていた。

一八　仙雲は船が博多を出た時から、いつも仰向けに横たわり、口を開けていた。そうしていることに依って船暈いを避けられると思い込んでいるらしかった。蒼い顔の中で髯の延びたのが目立ち、時々開いている口から大きい吐息が洩れるのが聞こえた。そんな弱り方はしていたが、眼だけは行賀と違って不遜だった。じろりと相手をねめつけるように見た。

一九　「何が可笑しいのだ」

いい気なものだ so optimistic; how self-complacent.　にこりともしないで without even a little smile.　日本でもっとも新しい知識人とされている真備を、物の数ともしない仙雲の傲岸な言葉に at the arrogant words of Sen'un who completely discounted (gave no importance to) Makibi, considered to be the newest intellectual in Japan.　半ば反感と半ば驚きとを感じた [Gyōga] felt partly antagonized and partly surprised.

20.　海色が浅緑になった騒ぎも黄濁した驚きも either to the commotion when the color of the sea changed to light green or the surprise when it became muddy yellow.　〜を受けつけない to reject (as with one's system rejecting certain types of food); make no response to 〜.　揚子江 Yangzi River.　引き潮のため船が砂上に置き去りにされて、動けなくなった時 when, due to the ebbing tide, the boats were stranded on the sand and unable to move.　見る影もなく痩せた体を遣うようにして船尾の方へ運んでいった creeping along, [Sen'un] carried his now unrecognizably lean body toward the stern.　異国の洋々たる川の広がりに目を遣り casting his eyes toward the expanse of the vast river in a foreign land.

21.　無事に唐土を踏んだ遣唐使の一行 the group of envoys who safely set foot on Tang soil.　都長安 Chang'an, the capital. It is now known as Xi'an (西安, J. Seian).　玄宗皇帝 Xuanzong, the sixth Tang emperor, r. 712-756. Particularly remembered in Japan for a love affair with Yang Guifei celebrated in the "Song of Everlasting Lament" (長恨歌; J. Chōgonka) by Bo Juyi (白居易; J. Hak' Kyoi).　〜に謁見した had an audience with 〜.　名門の出 coming from a distinguished background, a reference to Kiyokawa being son of Fusasaki, who was son of Fuhito. Fuhito compiled the Yōrō Ritsuryō, founded Kōfukuji, and established a privileged relationship with the imperial household by sending a daughter to Mon'mu (文武天皇) and another to Shōmu (聖武天皇).　容姿端麗、立居振舞は閑雅であった [Kiyokawa] was of an elegant appearance and his deportment was graceful. 立居振舞 (立ち居振る舞い) is a fixed phrase, 立居 meaning how one sits or stands and 振舞 how one carries oneself.　有義礼儀君子の国より使臣来ると激賞し highly praised them [Kiyokawa, Makibi, and so forth] saying that "envoys have come from the kingdom of principle and decorum." 礼 and 儀 both meant decorum, the former referring to the larger kind and the latter to the smaller.　清川、真備、古麻呂の肖像を描かせて、これを蕃蔵の中に納めさせるという款待（歓待）ぶりであった his [Xuanzong's] welcome was such that he ordered portraits of Kiyokawa, Makibi, and Komaro and had them stored in the foreign treasury. The character 蕃 here means foreigners as in 玄蕃寮（げんばりょう, the Bureau of Buddhism and Aliens) under the Ritsuryō system in Japan.

行賀が訊くと、仙雲は、

「雨雲が自分を避けて行くという考え方が可笑しかったのだ。いい気なものだ」

と、彼はにこりともしないで言った。行賀は、日本で最も新しい知識人とされている真備を、物の数ともしない仙雲の傲岸な言葉に半ば反感と半ば驚きとを感じた。

二〇　行賀が航海中、仙雲と話したのは、この時だけだった。仙雲は胃が悪いらしく、他の者全部が船暈いから立ち直っても、彼だけは死んだように横たわっていた。海色が浅緑になった騒ぎも黄濁した驚きも彼は受けつけなかった。そして船が揚子江にはいり、引潮のため船が沙上に置き去りにされて、動けなくなった時、彼は初めて見る影もなく痩せた体を這うようにして船尾の方へ運んで行った。そして異国の洋々たる川の拡がりに眼を遣り、いつまでも、その大きい不遜な眼を黄濁した水の面から離さなかった。

二一　無事に唐土を踏んだ遣唐使の一行は、その年の終りに都長安に辿り着いて、玄宗皇帝に謁見した。時に清河は四十七歳であった。

大使藤原清河は名門の出で、容貌端麗、立居振舞は閑雅であった。有義礼儀君子の国より使臣来ると激賞し、清河、真備、古麿の肖像を描かせて、これを蕃蔵の中に納めさせるという款待振りであった。

玄宗皇帝は、清河、真備等を見て、

22. **養老元年の第八回の遺唐使派遣** the 717 dispatch of the eighth mission.
阿部仲麻呂 (698/701-770). Went to Tang China in 717, on the same mission with
Kibi no Makibi and Genbō, and served its court. His wish to return in 733 was not
granted. He set out for a return journey in 753 with Kiyokawa and others. Ship-
wrecked, he returned to China and ended his life there.

23. **五十の坂を越えており** having passed the hilltop of age fifty—*it was considered downhill from fifty on.*　　**言語、立居振舞悉く唐人のそれになりきってい
た** his speech and manners had completely assimilated with, i.e., had become in-
distinguishable from, those of the Tang people.　　**行き方を異にして** choosing a
different course.　　**進士科の試験** government service examination.　　**左春坊司
経局校書** *roughly put,* head official of the crown prince's palace and clerk of the
library.　　**〜を振出(振り出し)に** starting out as 〜.　　**異数の出世をして**
having gone through rare promotions.　　**いまや衛尉卿の官にあって** now holding the office of director of the palace gate guards. 衛尉 was one of the nine 卿
(court ministers) established in the Qin dynasty.　　**従四品上** Junior Fourth Order,
Upper Grade. There were nine court officials, each dividing into senior and junior,
or further into upper and lower.　　**この国の器械文物の政令を一手に掌握してい
る唐朝高級官吏の一人** one of the top Tang government officials who held sway
over government ordinances relating to technology and culture in the country.

24. **再度入唐した** entered Tang China for the second time.

25. **玄宗の命に依って** at Xuanzong's order.　　**遺唐使の一行を〜を巡覧せし
めた** [Nakamaro] had the envoys tour 〜. The object of the verb 'tour' is 一百十
坊のうちの重だった幾つか; see the following two notes.　　**儒教、道教、仏教の
経典安置の堂宇である三教殿を初めとして** starting with/including the Hall of
the Three Teachings, which is the building that houses the scriptures of Confucian-
ism, Daoism, and Buddhism.　　**東西両街を埋める一百十坊のうちの重だった
幾つか** a number of the more important of the 110 monasteries that occupied both
eastern and western parts of the capital.

26. **五年の正月** the first month of the fifth year of Tenpyō (733).　　**唐朝の新年
の賀筵** the New Year's party at the Tang court. 賀筵 literally means 'celebratory
[seats on] bamboo mats.'　　**席次を新羅の使臣と争い** competing with the envoys
from Silla over seating arrangements.　　**ついに諸外国使臣のうちでは、最上位
の席を占めるに至った** finally came to occupy the highest seat (if only) among
envoys from various foreign countries.　　**これなども仲麻呂の力に負うところ
が多かった** this among other things owed much to Nakamaro's influence.

　長安には曾て養老元年の第八回の遣唐使派遣の時、玄昉や真備たちと入唐し、そのまま三十六年
この国に留まっている安倍仲麻呂がいた。

二三　仲麻呂は入唐した時は二十歳だったが、今は既に五十の坂を超えており、身には唐衣を纏い、言語、
立居振舞悉く唐人のそれになりきっていた。彼は他の留学生たちとは行き方を異にして、大学に入り、
そこを卒業すると進士科の試験を受けて、官吏となり、左春坊司経局校書を振出しに他国人としては
異数の出世をして、いまや衛尉卿の官にあって従四品上の位階を持っていた。この国の器械文物の政
令を一手に掌握している唐朝高級官吏の一人であった。

二四　仲麻呂と副使真備は同じ年の入唐留学生であったが、一人はそのまま唐土に留まって高官となり、
一人は帰朝して、こんど遣唐副使として、再度入唐したわけである。

二五　仲麻呂は玄宗の命に依って、遣唐使の一行を儒教、道教、仏教の経典安置の堂宇である三教殿を
初めとして、東西両街を埋める一百十坊のうちの重だった幾つかを巡覧せしめた。そうしているう
ちにその年は暮れた。

二六　五年の正月には、唐朝の新年の賀筵に、清河、古麿、真備等は出席し、その席次を新羅の使臣と
争い、ついに諸外国使臣のうちでは、最上位の席を占めるに到った。これなども仲麻呂の力に負うと
ころが多かった。

27. 帰国の途に上ることになっていた [the embassy] was expected to start out on a return journey.　　勧めを受けて accepting the encouragement [of Makibi and others].　　長い在唐生活を打ち切り bringing to a close his long stay in Tang China.　　日取りが決定すると when the date [of the return journey] was determined.　　詩を日本の使節に賜り [Emperor Xuanzong] deigned to give a poem to the Japanese envoys.　　朝臣を遣わして一行を揚州まで送らせることになった he would dispatch court vassals to accompany the envoys as far as Yangzhou.

28. 長安を辞した [the envoys] excused themselves from / left Chang'an.　　寺坊 temple building.　　ある程度唐語を解するようになっており [Gyōga and Sen'un] had come to understand the Tang speech to some extent.　　唐人の風俗習慣にも漸く慣れようとしていた were beginning to be familiar with Tang people's customs and manners as well.　　揚州まで送ることにした decided to accompany [the envoys] as far as Yangzhou.　　鑑真（鑑真）Jianzhen, 688-763. Tang priest who introduced the Ritsu sect of Buddhism to Japan and founded the temple Tōshōdaiji (唐招提寺) in Nara. He decided to go to Japan at the request of Japanese monks sent to Tang China in 732. After five unsuccessful attempts and the loss of his sight, he finally reached Japan in 753, and on arrival in Nara in the following year founded an ordination platform at Tōdaiji (東大寺) to begin his work. Jianzhen is the main character in Inoue Yasushi's 『天平の甍』 (てんぴょうのいらか, 1957; tr. Roof Tile of Tenpyō, 1975).　　一行とともに……謦咳に接すること to meet Jianzhen, the high priest of Yanguang Temple in Yangzhou, who was to cross the sea to Japan with the envoys. 謦 and 咳 both meaning "cough," 謦咳に接する is a rhetorical expression for directly hearing someone speak, i.e., to speak with, or meet, someone.

29. 乗船地蘇州 Suzhou, the place of embarkation.　　判官布勢人主 Fuse no Hitonushi, the third rank envoy.　　鑑真およびその従者（じゅうしゃ; arch. ずさ）の一団は第二船に配された it was arranged that the party of Yanzhen and his followers would embark on the second boat.

30. 四船 the four boats.　　忽ち instantly; in no time.　　暴風雨 a violent rain storm.　　〜に遇(あ)う to encounter 〜　　紀州に漂着し drifted to Kii province (present day Wakayama and southern Mie prefectures)　　薩摩の海浜に打ち上げられ was washed ashore at Satsuma province (present day western Kagoshima prefecture).　　これら三船に乗っていたものはともかく日本の土を踏むことはできた those who embarked on these three boats, whatever their condition, were at least able to step on Japan's soil.

その年の秋、一行は帰国の途に上ることになっていた。仲麻呂の帰国が決まったのは春である。真備等の勧めを受けて、仲麻呂も長い在唐生活を打ち切り、遣唐使節の一行と共に帰国することになったのである。遣唐使一行の帰国の日取りが決定すると、玄宗皇帝は、詩を日本の使節に賜わり、朝臣を遣わして一行を揚州まで送らせることになったのである。

一行が長安を辞したのは六月である。行賀と仙雲は、入唐以来これまで、長安の寺坊の一つに住んでいた。この期間に二人はある程度唐語を解するようになっており、唐人の風俗習慣にも漸く慣れようとしていた。遣唐使一行が長安を去る時、仙雲はそのまま長安に留まったが、行賀は一行を揚州まで送ることにした。一行と共に渡日することになっている揚州延光寺の高僧鑒真の謦咳に接することがその主な目的であった。

一行は揚州に行って鑒真を迎え、それから乗船地蘇州に向かった。彼等が四船に分乗して蘇州を出発したのは十一月十五日であった。

第一船には清河、第二船には古麿、第三船には真備、第四船には判官布勢人主が乗った。仲麻呂は第一船に、鑒真およびその従者の一団は第二船に配された。

四船は海にはいると忽ち暴風雨に遇い、このうち吉備真備の乗った第三船は紀州に漂着し、第二、第四の二船は薩摩の海浜に打ち上げられ、これら三船に乗っていた者はともかく日本の土を踏むこと

南方に吹き流されて安南に漂着した [the first boat, on which Nakamaro had embarked,] was blown to the south and drifted to Annam. 安南 (*Ch.* An'nan), "Pacify the South," was the name of a border defense base placed by Tang China in north Vietnam and eventually gave its name to the entire region of Annam. 　従うものの多くは土人に害されるという不運なくじを引いた [the boat] drew the unlucky lot of having many of his followers harmed (i.e., killed) by the natives. 土人 is a discriminatory term no longer used. 　清河、仲麻呂等は辛うじて生命は完うしたが…… Kiyokawa, Nakamaro, and others just barely survived, but had to set foot on Tang soil again. 生命を完うする（全うする）means to live one's life to full term.

31. 仲麻呂等の乗船が覆没した噂が、長安の町には流れていた rumor ran in the streets of Chang'an that the boat Nakamaro and others were on had capsized and sunk.

32. 李白 (Li Bo) 701-762. Tang poet and wanderer who loved wine. He served Xuanzong's court for three years. 　～を弔う詩一篇 a piece of poetry lamenting the death of ～. 　日本晁卿…… Minister Chao of Japan leaves the imperial capital / A single sailboat circles around the mountain of immortals / The bright moon does not return but sinks into the emerald sea / The melancholy hue of white clouds fills the hills of green phoenix trees. 　晁卿 Abe no Nakamaro went by the alias 晁衡 (Chao Heng; *J.* Chōkō) in China. At the time he left, he held the post of 衛尉卿 (police chief; *Ch.* weiweiqing). Thus he was called 晁卿 with the honorary suffix. 　征帆 the sails of a voyaging ship, a voyaging sailboat. 　蓬壺 "the Peng jar," another name for Hōraizan (蓬莱山; *Ch.* Penglaishan), an imaginary, jar-shaped, water-surrounded mountain where immortals are said to dwell. Believed to be located in Bohai, it was also sometimes associated with Japan. 　明月 the bright moon; the full moon of the fifteenth night by the lunar calendar. *This allusion to Nakamaro is especially resonant because his other alias in China was* 仲満, *which suggests* 仲秋明月 *(full moon of the fifteenth day of the eighth month) and* 満月 *(full moon).* 　蒼梧 （そうご、あおぎり）(1) "blue-green paulownia," Chinese parasol tree / phoenix tree / *filmiana planaifolia*; commonly written 青桐 （あおぎり）in Japanese. (2) the mountain in Hunan province where Emperor Xun, one of the mythical early Chinese rulers, is said to have died. 　碧 in 碧海 and 蒼 in 蒼梧 are different shades of blue or blue-green. *The text quotes the poem in the yomikudashi style (*訓み下し*), with the Japanese word order and supplementary kana. The original runs as follows, with the rhyme on* 都, 壺, *and* 梧:
日本晁卿辞帝都。征帆一片繞蓬壺。明月不帰沈碧海。白雲愁色満蒼梧。
字 male alias, which was given at the time a boy reached majority and used from then on as an adult name. 　その恩恵に浴さなかった [Kiyokawa, Nakamaro, and others] did not bask in (were not privileged to enjoy) the benefits [of Komaro's influence over rain clouds]. 　ある感慨を以て with a certain emotion / sentiment.

はできたが、清河、仲麻呂の乗った第一船は、南方に吹き流されて安南に漂着した。そして従う者の多くは土人に害されるという不運なくじを引いた。清河、仲麻呂等は辛うじて生命は完うしたが、再び唐土を踏まねばならなかった。

一行と揚州で別れた行賀が、長安に帰りついたのは翌六年の夏であった。その頃、仲麻呂の乗船が覆没した噂が、長安の町には流れていた。

それから二、三ヵ月したある日、仙雲は外出先から帰ると、どこで手に入れたのか、詩人李白の仲麻呂を弔う詩一篇を紙に記したものを行賀に示した。

晁卿は仲麻呂の字である。征帆一片蓬壼ヲ遶ル。明月帰ラズ碧海ニ沈ム。白雲愁色蒼梧ニ満ツ。

日本晁卿帝都ヲ辞ス。

行賀は、こんども亦雨雲は真備を避けて通り、清河、仲麻呂等はその恩恵に浴さなかったことを、ある感慨を以て思った。

併し、それから更に半歳余を経て、清河と仲麻呂は、漸く強い夏の陽射しが九街十二衢の楡の並木に散り始めた長安の都に姿を現したのである。勝宝七年六月のことである。仲麻呂は再び官に就き、清河は名を河清と改めて唐朝に仕えた。

行賀や仙雲は、遭難前の清河や仲麻呂とは話す機会もなかったが、彼等が二度目に長安に現われてからは、時にこの二人の先輩と顔を合わせる機会があった。行賀は親しく彼等と話すことはなかった

33. それから更に半歳余を経て a little over another half year later.　　九街十二衢 the large and small streets of Chang'an.　　楡の並木 elm trees lining the streets. 勝宝七年 755.　　仲麻呂は再び官につき、清河は名を河清と改めて唐朝に仕えた Nakamaro took a governmental office once again, and Kiyokawa, under the new name Kasei (*Ch.* He Qing), served the Tang court.

34. 遭難 disaster; shipwreck.　　臆面もなく unabashedly; brazenfacedly.　　役所 government office.　　私宅 private home.　　消息に通じていて being well informed.

35. 今までの経歴上何ら異とするに当たらなかったが [that Nakamaro took an office] was nothing strange in view of his previous record.　　彼に再び日本へ帰国する意志のないこと that he [Kiyokawa] had no intention of returning to Japan again.　　語気烈しく罵倒した [Sen'un] condemned [Nakamaro and Kiyokawa] with a fierce tone.

36. 併し、と言って、彼は真備を尊敬しているわけでもなかった however, it was not that he therefore respected Makibi, either; this did not mean that he respected Makibi; that didn't make him respect Makibi. と言って (followed by a negative) is short for だからといって.　　真備の話が出ると when the topic of Makibi surfaced. 「雨雲か！」 "That 'rain clouds' man!"; "Rain clouds, indeed!" 微かに軽べつが含まれていた there was a hint of contempt [in those words]. 生得のものであると見做して regarding [Makibi's good luck] as his innate quality.　　仏陀の教えとは無縁な人間と見ているようであった seemed to see [Makibi] as a man who had no relationship with the teachings of the Buddha.

37. 強ち理解できなくはなかった it was not necessarily the case that [Gyōga] failed to understand [Kiyokawa's taking a government post or Nakamaro's long-term stay in Tang China].　　人命を犠牲にしてなされる遣唐使の派遣ということに toward the dispatch of the embassy to Tang China that was undertaken at the cost of human lives.　　多少の疑問を持たないわけには行かなかった it was impossible not to feel a measure of doubt.　　日本の為政者への暗黙の抗議のようなものとして as something like a silent protest again Japanese rulers.　　この国で地位を得ている仲麻呂が、何も危険を冒して故国へ帰る必要のない気持ち the feeling of Nakamaro, who had gained a position in this country, that he need not risk his life returning to his old country.

が、仙雲の方は、臆面もなく、二人を役所や私宅に訪ねて行き、彼等の消息に通じていて、それをよく行賀に語ってくれた。

三五　仲麻呂が官に就いたことは今までの経歴上何ら異とするに当らなかったが、当然行賀と仙雲の間には一つの問題として論じられた。清河の仕官も、彼に再び日本へ帰国する意思のないことを示しているもののように見えた。仙雲はそういう二人を気烈しく罵倒した。清河も仲麻呂も、結局は駄目な人間だ」

三六　しか併し、と言って、彼は真備を尊敬しているわけでもなかった。真備の話が出ると、

「雨雲か！」

と、彼は言った。その言葉には微かに軽蔑が含まれていた。仙雲は真備の幸運を、彼の生得のものであると見做して、仏陀の教えとは無縁な人間と見ているようであった。

三七　行賀は清河の仕官も、仲麻呂の仕官も、強ち理解できなくはなかった。そして人命を犠牲にして為される遣唐使の派遣という事に多少の疑問を持たないわけには行かなかった。こんどの二人の唐朝への仕官は、日本の為政者への暗黙の抗議のようなものとして、行賀の心には映っていた。

この国で地位を得ている仲麻呂が、何も危険を冒して故国へ帰る必要のない気持は判ったが、併し、「日本人が日本の土を踏もうとする心を失った時はもうお終いだ。

それに反撥（反発）するものをも感じた [Gyōga] found himself reacting with antipathy toward it [Nakamaro's feeling].　殊に清河が遣唐大使の職責を忘れて、唐朝に仕えることに対しては especially about Kiyokawa serving the Tang court, forgetting his official responsibility as ambassador of the Tang mission.　真っ向から反対したかった [like Sen'un, Gyōga] felt like expressing downright opposition.

38.「だが、おれも当分は帰らんな」 "But I won't go home either for some time." 命が幾つあっても足りない no matter how many lifetimes I have, it's not enough for me.　例のぎろりとした眼で with his usual glaring eyes; with glaring eyes that were typical of him.　人を恋うるに似た情熱的な光を仙雲はその眼に持っていた Sen'un had in his eyes a passionate light that resembled [that in the eyes of one] in love with a woman. 恋うるに似た is slightly literary with the participial form 恋うる instead of the more modern 恋う.　彼を時々狂人のように見せていた [fatigue from fierce daily study since coming to China] made him sometimes look like a madman.

39. 唐僧の衣を纏っていた donned the robe of a Tang priest.　それまでの、入唐僧の総てがそうであったように北京の西南七十里の地点にある五台山を目指していた [Gyōga], as was the case with all the previous Japanese monks who entered Tang China, was headed for Mount Wutai located seventy li southwest of the north city. 北京, separate from today's Peking, was the Tang dynasty alias for Taiyuan (太原) in today's Shanxi province. 五台山, one of the great holy places of Chinese Buddhism, is a cluster of five flat peaks in northeast Shanxi province.　それまでの……そうであったように is an adverbial phrase modifying 目指していた. Tentatively ignore the rhythmical comma after それまでの and tentatively place a grammatical comma after そうであったように.　これといった当ては持っていず having no particular expectations / plans.　ひとまず揚州の開眼寺に行ってみるということであった [Sen'un], Gyōga understood, would as a preliminary step go to the Kaiyan temple in Yangzhou.　杏花と梨花 plum blossoms and pear blossoms.　いっせいに咲き出そうとしていた were about to bloom all at once.

40. 第十回の遣唐使派遣で、日本が得たもっとも大きいもの the greatest gain Japan made from the tenth mission to Tang.　鑑真に依って初めて戒律は日本に伝わった by Jianzhen the Buddhist precepts were for the first time brought to Japan.

また一方ではやはりそれに反撥するものをも感じた。殊に清河が遣唐大使の職責を忘れて、唐朝に仕えることに対しては仙雲と同様真向から反対したかった。

「だが、俺も当分は帰らんな」

と仙雲は一番最後に言った。

「知らなければならぬことがいっぱいある。生命が幾つあっても足りない」

仙雲は例のぎろりとした眼で行賀を見詰めた。人を恋うるに似た情熱的な光を仙雲はその眼に持っていた。入唐以来の日々の烈しい勉学の疲労が、彼を時々狂人のように見せていた。

それから半年程して、行賀、仙雲の二人は同時に長安を発って西と東に別れた。二人とも唐僧の衣を纏っていた。行賀はそれまでの、入唐僧のすべてがそうであったように北京の西南七十里の地点にある五台山を目指していた。仙雲の方はこれといった当ては持っていず、ひとまず揚州の開元寺に行ってみるということであった。天平勝宝八年（西紀七五六年）の春のことで、長安の郊外には杏花と李花がいっせいに咲き出そうとしていた。

　　第十回の遣唐使派遣で、日本が得た最も大きいものは、鑑真に依って初めて戒律は日本に伝わった。そして鑑真の他にも、古麿、真備等と一緒に渡日した高僧鑑真であった。彼に随行した僧侶たち

仏舎利 the Buddha's ashes.　　律、天台の経疏類 annotated texts of Ritsu and Tendai sect Buddhism. 疏 is pronounced そ in the usual sense of document but しょ in the sense of 義解（ぎげ）, explication of old texts.　　王義之 Wang Yizhi (321-379), calligrapher who perfected the three standard styles (clerical, cursive, and grass). He greatly influenced the calligraphy of Nara and Heian Japan. 真蹟 autograph (calligraphy in Wang Yizhi's own hand).　　彼等によって携行された brought by them [Tang priests who accompanied Yanzhen to Japan].

41. 日本に於いては in Japan if not in China; nearly the same as 日本において, except with selective emphasis.　　高元度 dates unknown. A Nara government official, who was sent to Tang China in 759 for the purpose of bringing home Fujiwara no Kiyokawa.　　渤海 see no. 5 above.　　時恰も precisely at that moment. 安禄山の乱 the Rebellion of An Lushan, 755. Due to conflict over control of the central government with the brother of Yang Guifei (Xuanzong's favorite consort), An Lushan, the "barbarian" leader of Iranian and Turkish descent, rebelled and captured Luoyang (considered to be the eastern capital), then Chang'an (the capital), causing Xuanzong to flee to Sichuan. Xuanzong's discontented soldiers executed Yang Guifei and her brother, and he eventually abdicated in favor of one of his sons. An Lushan was killed by his own son in 757, but the rebellion dragged on till 763. 時の皇帝粛宗には謁見できなかった was unable to have an audience with Suzong, the then emperor.　　勅が下された an imperial message was issued. *The paragraph that follows this sentence summarizes the content of the message.*

42. こんどの使者の要請によって清河は日本に帰したいが although we wish to return Kiyokawa to Japan at the request of the messenger sent this time.　　いまだに国内の残賊平らがず、その行程に困難が多く because the remaining rebels are not yet pacified and many hardships are expected in the process.　　清河の帰国は他日を期さなければならぬ we must look forward to another day for Kiyokawa's return.　　高元度もよろしく南路をとって帰るように Kō Gendo, too, should take [for safety's sake] a southern route home. よろしく(properly, as one thinks fit), when followed by an imperative as in よろしく～するように or よろしく～すべし, means "should" or "it behooves."　　空しく日本に引き上げて行った returned to Japan in vain.　　帰国の気配は見られなかった there was no sign of [Kiyokawa] returning to Japan.

が日本に入り、仏舎利を初め、律、天台の経疏類、仏像、王義之の真蹟などが彼等に依って携行された。

四一　大使藤原清河が唐に留まったまま帰らないことは、日本に於ては大きい問題になった。

それについての対策が一つの形となって現われたのは、天平宝字三年（西紀七五九年）に、高元度が藤原清河を迎える大使として渤海の船によって送られて唐に来たことである。時恰も安禄山の乱に際して、高元度は時の皇帝粛宗には謁見出来なかった。併し、彼が唐に留まっている間に勅が下された。

四二　こんどの使者の要請によって清河は日本に返したいが、未だに国内の残賊平がず、その行程に困難が多く、清河の帰国は他日を期さなければならぬ。高元度もよろしく南路をとって帰るように——こういう内容のものだった。

高元度は三年唐に留まったが、使命を果たさず空しく日本に引き上げて行った。その後も清河の帰国の気配は見られなかった。

四三　行賀が勉学の旅から長安に帰ってきたのは天平宝字六年（西紀七六二年）の夏である。第十一回目の遣唐使入唐の噂を伝え聞いて、その船便で故国へ帰ろうと思ったのである。入唐後十年の歳月が経ち、行賀は三十四歳になっていた。

44. 企て plan.　即ち namely; that is to say.　淳仁天皇 733-765, *r.* 758-764.
Also known as Awaji Haitei (淡路廃帝), "deposed emperor on Awaji," because he
was dethroned and banished to Awaji island when the uprising of Fujiwara no Nakamaro (藤原仲麻呂) was pacified. Nakamaro opposed the female emperor Kōken
(孝謙天皇) and Priest Dōkyō (道鏡) in support of Jun'nin. See 孝謙天皇 in no. 1.
仲真人石伴 a Nara courtier; appointed ambassador to Tang China in 761 but the
boats never left.　今までの四艘が改められ二艘とされた The number of ships
was changed from four, as in the past, to two. Four ships were sent for the first time
in 717 and again in 733.　海上の風波烈しくついに出港の時機を失い⋯⋯中
止の巳むなきに至った Losing the right moment for setting sail because of the
violent winds and waves upon the sea, they were forced to abandon [the plan for the
761 mission]. The phrase 〜の巳むなきに至る (*lit.*) to come to a point where 〜
does not end; i.e., to be unable to avoid. Two missions were abandoned, one in 761
and another in 762. They had been appointed to transport military supplies at the
request of the Tang court.

45. ために for this reason; archaic sounding but same as そのために in meaning.
僧房の一つに在って staying in one of the monasteries.　明けても暮れても
day in day out.　写経に没頭した was absorbed in copying sutras.　旗亭に上る
to visit a "flag house," i.e., a drinking establishment, restaurant, or inn. In China
such a place put up what was called a "wine flag" (酒旗).　彼と盃（はい、さか
ずき）を交わした exchanged wine cups, i.e., drank, with him.　話らしい話を取
り交わしたのは that [the two] exchanged conversations worthy of the name, decent conversations.

46. 自分を慰するため to comfort him [Gyōga]　その席で at that meeting, on
that occasion.　唐人のそれのように、動きというもののない表情で with an
expression, like that of a Tang person, utterly still.　難破した百何十人かの人間
more than ten dozen (*lit.* one hundred and some tens of) people who were ship-
wrecked [with myself].　溺死する to drown.

事実、その頃日本では第十一回遣唐使派遣の企てが発表されていた。即ち淳仁天皇の天平宝字五年（西紀七六一年）十月、仲真人石伴が遣唐大使として任命され、船は今までの四艘が改められ二艘とされた。そして翌年四月仲真人石伴は節刀を賜わったが海上の風波烈しくついに出航の時期を失い、この第十一回の遣唐使の企ては中止の已むなきに至ったのであった。

行賀はために帰国の機会を掴むことができなかった。行賀は六年から七年へかけて、長安に留まり、僧坊の一つに在って明けても暮れても写経に没頭した。

この時期に行賀は一度だけ藤原清河と親しく語ったことがあった。珍しく清河に誘われて、旗亭に上り、彼と盃を交わしたのである。二人が話らしい話を取り交わしたのは、この時が初めてであった。

行賀は、旗亭へ上ってから、清河が自分を招いたのは、帰国の機会を失った自分を慰するためであるのを知った。

その席で、行賀は、何故清河が、本国から迎えの使者がやって来たのに帰らなかったかということを訊ねた。すると、彼は、唐人のそれのように、動きというもののない表情で、

「自分と一緒に難破した百何十人かの人間は、大方溺死するか、土人に殺されている。私が一人帰ったら、私の妻子は悦ぶが、彼等の妻子は何と思うだろう」

47. はっとして struck; surprised; alarmed.　挙措動作は相変わらず優雅であ
ったが although his deportment and motions were graceful as before.　その老齢
は覆うべくもなかった his advanced age was impossible to conceal.　昔の貴公
子の端麗さ the refinement / elegance of the noble prince that he was long ago.

48. 名は河清と唐人の名に改まっていたが although his name had changed to a
Tang name, He Qing.　皮膚の色も、眼の色も、既に彼は本来のものを失おう
としていた he was already about to lose the original [beauty of the] color of his
skin and the color of his eyes.　文部卿 Minister of Literary Affairs. The name
Mon'bushō (文部省) replaced the more usual Shikibushō (式部省, the Ministry of
Ceremonial) between 758 and 764 under Fujiwara no Nakamaro's sway.　正四位
下 Senior Fourth Rank, Lower Grade. In Japan under the Ritsuryō system there
were four royal orders at the top, followed by eight courtly ranks from First to
Eighth, and one initial rank at the bottom. Each of the eight ranks divided into Senior and Junior, and further into Upper and Lower. The initial rank was divided into
Greater and Lesser, then into Upper and Lower.　故国でも厚く遇せられ、唐朝
においても厚く用いられている一人の老人の顔 the face of an old man who
was treated warmly in his old country and also employed well in the Tang court.

49. 春明門 the name of a gate.　鎮南都護 governor in charge of peace-keeping
in the south, i.e., chief of Annam.　彼は曾て漂流者として赴いた地へ、今度は
統治者として赴こうとしていた he [Abe no Nakamaro] was about to wend his
way, this time as a governor, to the place where he had once gone as a [ship-
wrecked] drifter.　さして親しみを感じなかった did not feel particular inti-
macy / affinity.　もやは日本人でなく no longer a Japanese.　全くの唐の高
名な武人であり、官吏であり、文人であった he [Kiyokawa] was, through and
through, a well-known Tang military man, government official, and literati.

50. 正面から顔を合わせた directly faced him.　認めたのか認めないのか
whether or not [Nakamaro] recognized [Gyōga] as Japanese.　ほとんど反応を見
せないで hardly showing any response.

と短い言葉で言った。

行賀ははっとして清河の顔を見た。既に清河は六十歳に近く、挙措動作は相変わらず優雅であったが、その老齢は覆うべくもなかった。昔の貴公子の端麗さはその顔からは想像できなかった。皮膚の色も、眼の色も、既に彼は本来のものを失おうとしていた。

名は河清と唐人の名に改まっていたが、変わっているのは名ばかりではなかった。

清河は故国には帰らなかったが、日本では彼を入唐大使として取り扱っていた。唐に居る間に、故国に於て清河は文部卿に任じられ、位は正四位下に進んでいた。

行賀は、故国でも厚く遇せられ、唐朝に於ても厚く用いられている一人の老人の顔を、今までの清河の顔とは全く違ったものとして眺めた。

この年に行賀はまた春明門の付近で、安倍仲麻呂に出会った。仲麻呂が鎮南都護に任ぜられたという噂を耳にした直後であった。彼は曾て漂流者として赴いた地へ、こんどは統治者として赴こうとしていた。六十歳を幾つか過ぎたこの老日本人に、行賀はさして親しみを感じなかった。最早日本人ではなく、全くの唐の高名な武人であり、官吏であり、文人であった。仲麻呂の方は、彼を日本人と認めたのか認めないのか、

行賀は正面から仲麻呂と顔を合わせたが、仲麻呂の方は、彼を日本人と認めたのか認めないのか、行賀が頭を下げたのに対して殆ど反応を見せないで歩き去って行った。行路の唐人たちは、この唐朝

次々に道を譲っていた were seen giving way one by one [to this high official].

51. どこから見てもても全くの唐人になり切っているのに despite the fact that [Nakamaro] had become a perfect Tang person from whatever angle one looked at him.　　それでいて and yet, for being that.　　彼の周囲を埋めているどの唐人とも違っているのを感じた [Gyōga] felt that he [Nakamaro] differed from any of the Tang people who surrounded him.　　どこかにそのように感じさせるものがあった there was something somewhere that gave that impression.　　二、三間あとをついて following 2 or 3 meters behind him [Nakamaro]; *a great show of respect.*　　一丁（一町）a block, approximately 109 meters.　　どこが唐人と違うか見定めてみたい誘惑を感じた [Gyōga] felt the temptation to ascertain where Kiyokawa differed from Tang people.

52. 帰国を思い立った determined to go home to Japan.　　果たさず not succeeding.　　唐の辺境にその老い先短い身を運ぼうとしている was about to carry himself in his advanced age (*lit.*, with not too many years to look forward to as he continues to age) to the Tang borderland.　　姿態 posture.

53. 憑かれたようにして as if bewitched / possessed.　　勉学と写経に費やした spent [the fifteen years] in studying and copying sutras.　　唯識 short for 唯識宗, another name for 法相宗 (ほっそうしゅう), the "mind only" sect practiced at 興福寺 (こうふくじ), 法隆寺 (ほうりゅうじ) and 薬師寺 (やくしじ).　　法華 short for 法華宗 (ほっけしゅう), the Tendai sect.

54. 西明寺 founded in 658 by Priest Xuanzhuang (玄奘, *J.* Genjō) in Chang'an at the order of Emperor Gaozong (高宗, *J.* Kōsō).　　牡丹 tree peony.　　～に没頭した was absorbed in.

の高官に対して、次々に道を譲っていた。

五一　行賀は、仲麻呂がどこから見ても全くの唐人になり切っているのに、それでいて、彼の周囲を埋めているどの唐人とも違っているのを感じた。どこが違っているか判らなかったが、どこかにそのように感じさせるものがあった。行賀は、仲麻呂の二、三間あとをついて一丁程歩いた。どこが唐人と違うか見定めてみたい誘惑を感じたのであるが、ついにそれを発見することはできなかった。

五二　若し、変わるものがあるとすれば、それは彼の経歴であったかも知れない。留学生として入唐し、唐の官吏となり、一度は帰国を思い立ったが、果たさず、ついに唐の辺境にその老い先短い身を運ぼうとしている。そうした人の特殊な姿態の表情が、行賀の心を打ったのであるかも知れなかった。清河と語ったのは春であり、仲麻呂と出遇ったのは夏の初めであった。

五三　それから第十二回の遣唐使の一行が来るまでの十五年を、行賀は憑かれたようにして、勉学と写経に費した。前半七年は定州、武陵、蘇州等の幾つかの開元寺で過ごし、入唐当初の目的通り、唯識、法華両宗を学び、後半は長安の寺坊の一つを与えられて、そこに住した。

五四　行賀は長安に住するようになってからは、眼を悪くしているせいもあったが、殆ど外出しなかった。有名な西明寺の牡丹さえも彼は知らなかった。明けても暮れても机に向かって経を写す仕事に没した。

写し得た was able to copy.　　五百余巻 over 500 scrolls.　　～に及ぼうとして
いた [the number of the sutras] was about to amount to ～.　　さらに甚だしくな
り became even more striking.　　彼の躯を二つに折って [his far-gone near-
sightedness] causing him to bend his body double.　　経典をなめるような姿勢を
取らせた made him assume a posture such that it seemed as if he were licking the
pages of a sutra.

55. 安南都護、安南節度使として異境にあった who was in a foreign land as
governor of Annam (present-day Vietnam) and commander of its frontier guards.
没した died.　　その任を解かれ relieved of his duties.　　時の～ the then ～.
代宗 [emperor] Dai Zong (*r.* 765-80).　　潞州大都督 governor of Lu province.
～を贈られた was given the title of ～.

56. 渤海 see no. 5 above.　　行賀が耳にしたのは that Gyōga heard of it.　　幸運
に取り巻かれて surrounded by good fortune.　　他界した left this world [leav-
ing big, brilliant footsteps]　　彼が入唐した年から推算して estimating from
the year that Makibi entered Tang China.

57. ～から間もない時 not long afer ～.　　全く思いがけず wholly unexpect-
edly.

58. 揶揄 banter.　　行賀が学僧として名を出しかけていたので since Gyōga
was becoming known as a scholar priest.　　それに対する旧友としての素直な喜
びの表現と見てよかった it was fine to take [the first word Sen'un uttered] for an
expression of unfeigned joy he felt as an old friend.

頭した。彼が写し得た経典は五百余巻に及ぼうとしていた。生まれつきの猫背はさらに甚だしくなり、強度の近視は彼の躰を二つに折って、経典を嘗めるような姿勢を取らせた。

この十五年間に、幾つかの出来事があった。一つは神護景雲四年（西紀七七〇年）一月に安倍仲麻呂が歿したことであった。長く安南都護、安南節度使として異境にあった彼は、七十一歳の時その任を解かれ、長安へ帰って来たが、その翌々年歿したのである。時の代宗から潞州大都督を贈られた。

もう一つは、渤海の使者の口から聞いた吉備真備の死である。歿年は仲麻呂の死から数年経った宝亀六年のことで、行賀が耳にしたのは、その翌年のことであった。雨雲も自分を避けて行くと言った真備は、一生を幸運に取り巻かれて、輝かしい大きな足跡を残して他界したのであった。行賀は真備の年齢が、彼が入唐した年から推算して、八十歳を超えることを知った。

それからもう一つは、一緒に入唐した仙雲と二回遇ったことである。一回目は、仲麻呂の葬儀のあった年で、行賀が長安の寺坊の一つに移り住んでから間もない時であった。行賀は、全く思いがけず、仙雲の訪問を受けた。

「豪くなったな」

仙雲が口から発した最初の言葉はこれであった。幾らかは揶揄も含まれていたかも知れなかったが、行賀が学僧として名を出しかけていたので、それに対する旧友としての素直な悦びの表現と見てよかっ

風采はみすぼらしかった was shabby looking.　と言って格別生活には困っ
ている風でもなかった did not, despite that, particularly seem to be badly off.

59.　入唐翌々年別れて以来 since parting two years after arriving in Tang China.
夜を徹して all night through.　　足跡あますところないと言ってよいほど so
that one could say Sen'un's footsteps left no untrodden area.　　到るところ every-
where.　　峨眉山 (Mount Emei) in southwest Sichuan province (四川省) in China,
so called because two of the peaks are reminiscent of eyebrows. 峨眉, literally
moth's eyebrows (antennae), is a euphemism for beautiful eyebrows.　　～の消息
に詳しい to be well posted about / well informed on ～.　　普賢の浄土 Fugen's
dwelling place. 普賢 (*Skt:* Samantabhadra) is a bodhisattva ("one whose essence is
enlightenment"), who, along with Monju (*Skt:* Mañjuśrī), is associated with wisdom.
浄土 is a Buddhist pure land; 21 trillion pure lands are said to exist.　　その山地で
何年かを過ごしていた (Sen'un) had spent a few years in those mountains.

60.　部屋いっぱいを埋めている行賀が写した経巻の中に埋まって buried in
the midst of sutras Gyōga had copied, which filled the entire room.　　暁(明け方)
around dawn.　　と言って、それをけなす風でもなかった yet did not seem to be
critical of them [Gyōga's achievements], either.　　憑かれた眼をしていた had
eyes that looked possessed.　　何物かに憑かれなければ、そのような眼はでき
るものではなかった unless possessed by something, one could never have such
eyes.

61.　いつ機会が来るかもわからない帰国の事を話題にすると when [Gyōga]
mentioned a return voyage, of which no one knew when the chance might come.
大袈裟な big-gestured / exaggerated; from 袈裟 (けさ), a Buddhist surplice.
奇矯な言辞を弄する to play with, or enjoy using, eccentric rhetoric.　　甚だしく
なっていた had become extreme.

た。そのように行賀は友の言葉を受け取った。仙雲は風采は見すぼらしかったが、と言って格別生活には困っている風でもなかった。

仙雲はその晩行賀の寺に泊まった。夜を徹して二人は語った。入唐翌々年別れて以来会っていないほど、行賀は友が懐しかった。仙雲は足跡あますところないと言っていいほど、広い大陸の到るところを歩いていた。殊にまだ人の余り行かぬ峨眉山の消息に詳しく、普賢の浄土と言われるその山地では彼は何年かを過ごしていた。

二人は部屋いっぱいを埋めている行賀が写した経巻の中に埋まって、暁方短い睡りを取ったが、仙雲は、行賀の業績をたいして感心している風でもなく、と言って、それをけなす風でもなかった。一口に言えば無関心であった。仙雲は若い時と同じように憑かれた眼をしていた。何物かに憑かれなければ、そのような眼は出来るものではなかった。行賀には、彼が何に憑かれているか判らなかった。

行賀がいつ機会が来るかも判らない帰国の事を話題にすると、

「君はまだ日本に帰ることを考えているのか」

と言った。そしてその時だけ、仙雲は驚いたような顔をして、大袈裟な笑い声を立てた。そんなところは奇矯であった。もともと若い時から奇矯な言辞を弄する癖があったが、それが四十歳を過ぎている彼には甚だしくなっていた。

62. 寺を辞するとき when Sen'un was leaving the temple.　真先に訊くべきこ
とを [asked] what he [Gyōga] should have asked before anything else.　その時
になって口にすると when Gyōga mentioned it at this late point.　晁卿 Abe no
Nakamaro; see no. 32.

63. 彼が墓を詣りに来た仲麻呂と同じように like Nakamaro, whose grave
Sen'un had come to visit.　故国の心を喪いつつある人間 a man who was on
the way to losing the love of his old country.　栄達 recognition, worldly fame.
烈しく非難を浴びせた bombarded with harsh criticism.　それを口にしよう
として in the act of bringing this up.　何か憚られるもののあるのを感じてや
めた stopped, sensing a need for restraint.

64. そろそろ遣唐使派遣のことが耳に入り出した rumors of the dispatch of a
mission to Tang China began to be heard.　宝亀元年 770, the first year of Hōki
(770-780), the era immediately following Jingo Keiun (770-780).

65. 胡商の住む陋巷 poor, crowded streets where foreign tradesmen lived. In
Chinese, 胡 originally referred to areas north of China but it was also used as a
reference to foreign lands in general. Here we should be thinking about regions to
the west of China.　その容貌や年齢から推して guessing from [what he heard
about] the man's appearance and age.　果たしてその人物が仙雲であるか否か
を確かめに行ってみた [Gyōga] went there to ascertain whether or not that person
was in fact Sen'un.

66. 胡人 northern people; foreigners. See no. 65 above.

94　井上靖

寺を辞する時、門口まで送って行った行賀が、

「一体、何しに長安へ来たのか」

と、真先に訊くべきことを、その時になって口にすると、

「晁卿の墓を詣りに来た」

と仙雲は答えた。

仙雲もまた、彼が墓を詣りに来た仲麻呂と同じように、故国の心を喪いつつある人間のように、行賀には思われた。二人の違うところは、仲麻呂には栄達があったが、仙雲には全くそんなものはなかった。

行賀は、仙雲が曾て、仲麻呂と清河が日本に帰らないことに対して烈しく非難を浴びせたことのあったのを思い出したが、それを口にしようとして何か憚かられるもののあるのを感じてやめた。

次に行賀が仙雲に遇ったのは、そろそろ遣唐使派遣のことが、耳に入り出した宝亀七年の秋である。

この前来た時から更に七年の月日が経過していた。

行賀は、胡商の住む陋巷に一人の狂人のような日本人の僧侶が居るということを聞いた時、その容貌や年齢から推して、それが仙雲ではないかと思った。同じ噂を二度目に耳にした日、行賀はそこへ、果してその人物が仙雲であるか否かを確かめに行ってみた。雑多な服装をし、それぞれ異なった言語を話している胡人の店が立ち並んでいる一廓であった。

仙雲が道行く人々に呼びかけ何事かを呶鳴（怒鳴）っている姿を見た [Gyōga] saw Sen'un calling to passers-by and shouting something at them.　その姿は狂人としか解することはできなかった his appearance could only be understood as that of a madman.　喋っているのは胡族の言語であろうか possibly what Sen'un spoke was the language of a western people.

67. 異様な笑いを片頬に浮かべた gave a strange lopsided smile.　どういうものか for some reason.　曽て同じ留学僧であった友が狂っていないこと that his friend, who was once a fellow student monk, had not gone insane.

68. 一隅 a corner.　西域を経て天竺へ行く計画をたて having made a plan to go to India through the western regions. 天竺 is an archaic name for India.　彼に同行する胡人を求めているのであった Sen'un was looking for a foreigner [from the western regions] who would accompany him [to India].　ここ十数年来の for the past fifteen or sixteen years.

69. 釈尊 the Buddha; a respectful appellation.　仏教が発祥し栄えた国 the country where Buddhism originated and flourished; 発祥する literally means "to reveal a good omen."　砂塵 sand dust.　仙雲の印象は何か蓬々たるものだった the impression Sen'un gave had a hint of wildness. 蓬々 is a word that describes overgrown grass, unkempt hair, wildly rising smoke or vapor, or wild wind, from 蓬 （よもぎ, mugwort), a plant that grows to 1 meter.

人たちが、その陋巷には群れ集まっていた。

行賀はそこで、仙雲が道往く人々に呼びかけ何事かを叫喚っている姿を見た。なるほど、その姿は狂人としか解することはできなかった。喋っているのは胡族の言語であろうか、行賀には全然理解することはできなかった。

「仙雲！」

行賀が呼びかけると、仙雲は驚いて振り返ったが、直ぐ異様な笑いを片頬に浮かべた。その時、行賀はどういうものか、渡唐する船の中で、最初に会った時の仙雲の顔を思い出した。仙雲はゆっくりと、行賀の方へ歩み寄って来た。行賀は曽て同じ留学僧であった友が狂っていないことを知って安心した。

二人はその時、短い時間、その陋巷の一隅で立ち話をした。仙雲は西域を経て天竺へ行く計画をたて、彼に同行する胡人を求めているのであった。天竺行きは、ここ十数年来の彼の念願であり、過去に於ても、何回か、それを試みているということであった。

「釈尊の生まれた地を、仏教が発祥し栄えた国を俺は見たいんだ。お前だって見たいだろう。ただ、俺は本当にそうしようと思っているだけだ」

そう彼は言った。風の強い日で、あたりに砂塵が舞い上がっていたせいもあったが、仙雲の印象は

唐僧に依って海路が用いられていた the sea route was employed by Chinese monks.　あるいは彼が船に弱いということのためかも知れなかった it may perhaps have been because of the fact that he was not good with boats. *Sen'un was badly seasick on the way to China.*

70. 近く実現を見るかもしれない遣唐使派遣のこと the mission to Tang China that might materialize soon.　口調にはひそやかなものがあったが、その眼はつき放すように行賀を見ていた there was a calm in his tone, but his eyes regarded Gyōga with a sharpness that seemed to cast him off / refuse his approach. ひそやか describes a hushed, hidden state or movement.

71. 光仁天皇 709-781, *r.* 770-781. Tenji's grandson known as Shirakabe, became crown prince the day 称徳 (Shōtoku; ruled first as 孝謙 Kōken) died and became emperor two months later.　宝亀 (770-80), the era immediately following Jingo Keiun.　佐伯今毛人 (さえきのいまけびと, also pronounced さえきのいまえみし) 719-790. A Nara period courtier. He engaged in the building of Tōdaiji, Saidaiji, and Nagaoka Palace. He was appointed ambassador to Tang China in 775. Due to the weather, his boat returned to Kyūshū. When the second attempt was made, illness prevented his going. Rose to 参議 (さんぎ, councilor). Also served at different times as 民部卿 (みんぶきょう, Minister of Popular Affairs) and 大宰帥 (だざいのそち, governor of the provinces in Kyūshū with diplomatic and defense responsibilities).　大伴益立 (おおとものますたて, also ましたつ, ましたち) date unknown. Starting in 760, he participated in administering the Northeast as 鎮守軍監 (ちんじゅぐんげん, third-rank military officer, just below vice commander, of the office of Mutsu Pacification), then as 陸奥鎮守副将軍 (むつちんじゅふくしょうぐん, vice commander of the office of Mutsu Pacification). He was appointed vice ambassador to Tang China in 775, an office he did not fulfill.　節刀を持って carrying the ceremonial sword [bestowed by the emperor on the ambassador].　順風を得ずして not having been favored with good winds. 博多に帰るの巳むなきに到った (*lit.*) reached a point where there was no avoiding a return to Hakata, i.e., could not but return to Hakata.　いかなる事情があったのか due to some unknown circumstance.　副使益立は廃され Masutate, the vice ambassador, was discharged.　小野石根・大神末足 Nara courtiers.　両人がこれに替わった the two replaced Masutate as vice ambassadors.

72. 今毛人が病んだので because Imakebito fell ill.　一団を率いて進発した started out leading the group of envoys.

73. 藤原清河宛の書を携行していた carried a letter [from the Japanese court] addressed to Fujiwara no Kiyokawa. The original letter, written in kanbun, is here given in the 訓み下し (よみくだし) style.　汝 you.　使を絶域に奉じて sent to the farthest regions at imperial order.　久しく年序を経たり [you] have

何か蓬々たるものだった。天竺への道は何年か前から唐僧に依って海路が用いられていたが、彼が陸路を取ろうとしているのは、あるいは彼が船に弱いということのためかも知れなかった。

行賀は、彼の話を聞いたあとで、近く実現を見るかも知れない遣唐使派遣のことを話してみた。

すると、仙雲は、

「じゃあ、別れか。こんどは本当の別れだな」

と言った。口調にはひそやかなものがあったが、その眼はつき放すように行賀を見ていた。

行賀は、それから一カ月程して、再び仙雲をそこに訪ねたが、もう彼の姿はなかった。

第十二回遣唐使の人選の発表のあったのは、光仁天皇の宝亀六年（西紀七七五年）のことである。そして翌七年八月今毛人は節刀を持して船出したが、順風を得ずして博多に帰るの巳むなきに到った。そして如何なる事情があったのか、副使益立は廃され、新たに小野石根、大神末足の両人がこれに替わった。

佐伯今毛人を大使とし、大伴益立を副使とする旨が六月発表された。

副使益立は廃され、新たに小野石根、末足両副使が彼に替わって一団を率いて進発した。遣唐使の派遣は二十六年目のことであった。

翌八年六月大使今毛人が病んだので、石根、末足両副使が彼に替わって一団を率いて進発した。遣唐使の派遣は二十六年目のことであった。

幸い一行は無事唐土に着した。この時、石根は日本の朝廷からの藤原清河宛の書を携行していた。

汝使を絶域に奉じて、久しく年序を経たり、忠誠遠く著はれて、消息聞ゆるあり。故に今聘

spent many a long year.　忠誠遠く著われて (*lit.*) your loyalty has revealed itself far; your loyalty has been made known far [enough to reach the Japanese court]. 消息聞ゆるあり we have heard news of you.　故に今聘使に因りて therefore, now by a visiting messenger. 聘 can mean either "visit to inquire after someone's health" or "summon."　便ち之を迎へしむ so I have [the messenger] bring you home.　仍て絁一百匹、細布一百端、砂金大一百両を賜ふ thus, I bestow on you 2,000 yards of rough silk, 1,000 meters of narrow cloth, and 100 *ryō* of gold dust. 匹 is a unit of cloth length, approximately 11.4 meters in the Ritsuryō days. 端, another unit of cloth length, was half of 匹 later on but not necessarily in those days. 両 was a unit of weight based on the Chinese way of using 100 medium sized grains of millet to determine one 銖 (しゅ); 24 *shu* made one *ryō*.　よろしく努力して、使と共に帰朝すべし you should make efforts to return with the envoy. 相見んこと賖きに非ず not that we will see each other long hence. The kanji 賖 reads ショ, はるか, とおい, おぎのる, etc.　指多く及ばず I have many thoughts and fall short [of conveying all]; (*alternate reading*) many of my thoughts do not reach [you]. 指 here works in the same way as 旨 (purport; instructions).

74. この書を賜った時 when he received this epistle from the emperor. 賜る is the spontaneous/intransitive form of the transitive 賜ふ (たまう／たもう), to bestow.　在唐中 during his stay in Tang China.　次々に叙勲され having been conferred one rank (post) after another.　常陸守 governor of Hitachi province. Hitachi is the present northeast Ibaraki prefecture.　従三位に叙せられていた he had been promoted to Junior Third Order.

75. 長安に半年を過ごして after spending half a year in Chang'an. に in 長安 に is somewhat literary; in modern spoken Japanese it would be で.　遣唐使派遣のことがないままにいつか歳月は過ぎ years and months passed unmarked, with no news of a mission to Tang China.

77. 詔勅 imperial edict.　動静 moves.　無口な気難しい老人 an old man reticent and hard to please.　彼がいかなる考えを持っているか what kind of thoughts he had.

78. 嬉娘 (*Ch.*) Xiniang.

79. 自分の考えを行賀に洩らした let Gyōga know his thoughts. 洩らす from 洩る, to leak, is used when letting slip a hidden thought or a secret plan.

使に因て、便ち之を迎へしむ。仍て絁一百匹、細布一百端、砂金大一百両を賜ふ。宜しく努力して、使と共に帰朝すべし。相見ること賒きに非ず、指多く及ばず。

この書を賜わった時、清河は七十二歳であった。在唐中、彼は次々に叙勲され、常陸守を授けられ

従三位に叙せられていた。

石根等遣唐使の一行は長安に半歳を過ごして春の初めにそこを発つことになっていた。十月蘇州より帰国の船に乗るためであった。

行賀は勿論この遣唐使の一行と共に帰国するつもりでいた。初め入唐する時は、このように長く唐に居るつもりではなかったが、遣唐使派遣のことがないままにいつか歳月は過ぎ、年齢は五十歳になっていた。

詔勅を得た清河の動静は多くの人たちから注目されたが、清河は自分の意思というものを絶対に他人に覗かせなかった。この頃、清河は無口な気難しい老人になっており、誰も彼がいかなる考えを持っているか知ることはできなかった。

遣唐使一行が長安を去る数日前、行賀は突然清河の訪問を受けた。彼はこの時、嬉娘という二十歳の娘を連れていた。唐へ来てからこの国の女との間に出来た娘であった。

清河は、行賀の寺の一室で、初めて自分の考えを行賀に洩らした。

わしは故国に帰るには老い過ぎている I am too old to return home. わし, a corrupt form of わたくし, is still used dialectally or by older men with a degree of superiority. *Kiyokawa's speech here is deliberately stiff, in semi-indirect narration though in quotation marks.*　凡そものの進退には時というものがある as a rule, there is a timing to how things progress or retreat.　誰よりも汝に頼むのがいいと思うので since I think it better to trust her with you than anyone else. 汝 is archaic, though here without a great deal of incongruity because of the context; the rest of the speech is in modern Japanese.　いつもの気難しさを些かも和らげない表情で with an expression that did not in the least mitigate his usual moodiness.

80. 端麗な容貌と姿態 graceful/refined countenance and form.　貴女は日本の国を見たいのか *a speech, like Kiyokawa's daughter's response that follows, that slightly hints at a Japanese translation from an imaginary Chinese dialogue.*　父は、父と離れて住む気持ちを知らなければ不可ないというのです my father says I have to know how one feels living away from one's father. For the Japanese いけない, the kanji for 不可 (*Ch.* bu ke) were often used in earlier days, but the use here seems deliberate, hinting at a Chinese dialogue as it recalls the double negative kanbun construction like 不可不知（シラズンバアルベカラズ／シラザルベカラズ）.　わたし一人が恵まれすぎてはならぬというのでしょうか perhaps it means that I alone should not be too blessed.

81. 疑問を含めた言い方で (*lit.*) in an expression that contained a question; partly as a question.　彼が郷里に残してきた妻子のことを慮って thoughtful of his wife and children whom he had left at home.　清河の面に目を当てた cast his gaze on Kiyokawa's face.　木蘭 magnolia.　一人の気難しい老人として as a single difficult old man [rather than as the former ambassador to Tang China].

「わしは故国に帰るには老い過ぎている。凡そものの進退には時というものがあるが、帰国の時はすでにわしからは遠く去った。自分の代りに、この娘を日本に送りたい。誰よりも汝に頼むのがいいと思うので、今日ここへ伴って来た」

清河はいつもの気難しさを些かも和らげない表情で言った。

嬉娘は若い時の清河に似て、端麗な容貌と姿態を持っていた。彼女は父が話し終わると、黙って行賀の方へ頭を下げた。

「貴女は日本の国を見たいのか」

行賀が訊くと、

「父の国ですから勿論日本を見たいと思います。でも、そのために父と離れて住むのは嫌です。でも、父は、父と離れて住む気持を知らなければ不可ないと言うのです。わたし一人が恵まれ過ぎてはならぬというのでしょうか」

最後の言葉は疑問を含めた言い方で嬉娘の口から出た。清河は彼が郷里に残して来た妻子のことを慮って、嬉娘をもまた同じ立場に置こうとしているのかも知れなかった。

その時行賀は清河の面に眼を当てたが、耳の遠い彼には娘の言葉が通じなかったらしく、寺内の木蘭の木に視線を据えたまま、彼は一人の無表情な気難しい老人として坐っていた。

82. 招きを辞して declining the invitation [to return].　　素直に今の清河の心を解したかった wished to interpret Kiyokawa's present state of mind simply [without attempting to be analytical].　　帰国するに当たって at the time of his return to Japan.　　嬉娘を伴うことを清河に約した promised Kiyokawa that he would take Kijō. Cf. (1) 〜を伴う (to bring 〜); (2) 〜に伴う (to accompany 〜).

83. 厖大な経典類を携行した taking with him a colossal number of Buddhist scriptures.　　盗賊に監禁されるという不慮の出来事に遭遇し encountering the unexpected incident of being incarcerated by bandits.　　〜に亘って over; spanning. [The four boats had already started out] at two different times.

84. 茫然とした stunned, absent-minded. The kanji 茫 means spacious, uncontoured, and vague.　　身動き一つできない気持ちだった felt as if he could not stir an inch; felt stuck fast.　　揚子江上を夥しい難破船の破片が流れ漂うのを見た saw large pieces of debris from wrecked boats floating on the Yangzi river.

85. 揚子江上にあった船で大破、覆没したものその数を知らなかった among the boats on the Yangzi river, countless numbers were seriously damaged or listed and sunk.　　〜したものその数を知らなかった (lit.) as for those that [got shipwrecked], there was no knowing their number; a slightly archaic fixed phrase not requiring は after the topic.　　洋上で at sea.

86. どうにか満足な姿で in barely satisfactory form.　　船体を両断され the hull split in half.　　唐使趙宝英 Zhao Baoying, the emissary from Tang China. 舳部 the bow or stem of a boat, here the front half.　　肥前 the name of a province in Kyūshū, now Saga and Nagasaki prefecture.　　艫部 the bow or stem part of a boat, here the rear half.　　薩摩 the name of a province in Kyūshū, the western half of the present Kagoshima prefecture.

祖国の朝廷からの招きを辞して、彼は自分の代りに嬉娘を差し出そうとしている——行賀はただそんな風に素直にいまの清河の心を解したかった。行賀は帰国するに当たって、嬉娘を伴うことを清河に約した。

遣唐使の一行と一緒に嬉娘は長安を発ったが、行賀だけは仕事の関係で一月遅れて出発した。彼は日本へ持ち帰る経論で、どうしても写しておきたいものが残っていたのである。

厖大な経典類を携行した行賀は、蘇州へ向かう途中、盗賊に監禁されるという不慮の出来事に遭遇し、揚州へ辿り着いたのは予定より一月遅れた十一月の初め、蘇州へ着いたのは十一月の半ばであった。

四隻の遣唐使船は九月初めと十一月初めの二回に亙って既に進発していた。

茫然とした行賀は蘇州の開元寺にはいったまま身動き一つできない気持だった。蘇州に到着してから十日目に烈しい暴風雨があった。その後何日間か、行賀は毎日のように揚子江上を夥しい難破船の破片が流れ漂うのを見た。

この暴風雨のために、揚子江上にあった船で大破、覆没したものその数を知らなかったが、洋上でこの暴風雨に遇った遣唐使船二隻もまた例外ではなかった。

二船のうち一船はどうにか満足な姿で帰国することができたが、他の一船は船体を両断され、副使石根等三十八人と唐使趙宝英等三十五人は海に呑まれ、船の軸部は肥前に漂着、艫部は薩摩に漂着

87. 七十三歳を以て他界した passed away at age seventy-three.　安否が唐土に伝わっていなかった the news of whether the envoys were safe or not had not reached Tang China.

88. 清河から嬉娘のことを託されながら、それを果たしていなかった despite being trusted by Kiyokawa to care for Kijō, Gyōga had not fulfilled his responsibility.　重く心にのしかぶさっていた [her safety] had been weighing heavily on his heart.　幸運にも to her great fortune.　この上なく more than anything else; extremely.

89. 清河の墓前にそれを報ずるために in order to report [Kijō's safe arrival] before Kiyokawa's grave.　長安に向けて旅立ち setting out for Chang'an.　帰国の船便を得やすかった it was easier to find a shipping service for a return voyage.　しきりに帰国の情に駆られた was repeatedly driven by thoughts of returning.

90. 黄濁した muddy and yellow.　縹緲とした拡がり the vast, vague expansion.　渤海国 Bohai, see no. 5.　肥前松浦郡橘浦 a place name in Matsura (also pronounced Matsuura) county in Hizen province.　漂着した drifted.　延暦 the name of Kanmu's era, 782-806. In the 13th year of Enryaku (794), the capital moved to Kyōto, marking the beginning of the Heian era.　在唐期間 the period of his stay in Tang China.

91. 奈良興福寺 Kōfukuji (*hist.* Kōbukuji) in Nara; one of the seven largest temples in Nara and the center of Hossō sect Buddhism. See 2 above.

した。舳艫部共にそれぞれ何十人かの生存者を載せていたが、舳部の生存者中に、清河が自分の代りに故国に送った嬉娘も居た。

（七七九）行賀は蘇州の開元寺で宝亀十年を迎えた。そしてその年の春の終りに、藤原清河が昨年末に長安で七十三歳を以て他界したことを知った。この時はまだ遣唐使一行の安否が唐土に伝わっていなかったので、嬉娘の生死については、行賀も知らなければ、清河も知らなかったわけである。

（八八）嬉娘が日本の土を踏んだのを行賀が知ったのは、その年の夏であった。行賀は清河から嬉娘のことを託されながら、それを果たしていなかったので、それまで彼女の安否は重く心にのしかぶさっていたが、彼女が幸運にも日本へ着いたということは行賀の心をこの上なく明るくした。

（八九）行賀は清河の墓前にそれを報ずるために、直ぐ長安に向けて旅立ち、その年の暮長安に着いて、そこで半歳を過ごし、再び蘇州へ戻って来たのは十一年の暮であった。蘇州に居る方が帰国の船便を得やすかったからである。この頃行賀はしきりに帰国の情に駆られた。

（九〇）行賀は黄濁した揚子江の縹渺とした拡がりを見ながら更に三年の歳月を過ごした。

（九一）行賀が日本へ向かう渤海国の船に乗って、肥前松浦郡橘浦に漂着したのは延暦二年（西紀七八三年）の秋であった。時に、行賀五十五歳、在唐期間三十一年であった。

行賀は翌三年六月奈良興福寺に入った。

東大寺 also one of the seven largest in Nara and the center of the Kegon (*Ch.* Huayan) sect, founded at the order of Shōmu. See no. 3 above.　　唯識、法華両宗 の宗義 the religious doctrines of both the Hossō and Tendai sects.　　試問役を引 き受けて accepting the role of examiner.　　明一 (728-798) a Nara priest at Tōdaiji, known for criticizing Gyōga for failure to provide instant answers to his questions on religious doctrines.　　行賀と対座した sat face to face with Gyōga.

92. 日本の言葉を口にする to speak Japanese.　　答えるのが不自由でもあり、 億劫でもあった he not only found it difficult but felt too lazy to answer in Japanese.

93. 何刻か a few minutes. 刻 is a unit of time that corresponds to about two hours but also used to refer to an undefined passage of time.　　行賀の頭上に降っ た (*lit.*) [a stern voice] fell on Gyōga's head.　　久しく歳月を経て、学殖膚浅 having spent many long years [in China], your learning is skin-shallow. An alternate reading of 学殖膚浅 is 学植庸浅, your learning is mediocre and shallow.　　赤く 怒気を含んでいる (*lit.*) containing anger to redness, i.e., red with anger.　　茫然 として lost [as if in the wide sea].　　水を打ったように静かに堂内を埋めてい るのを見た saw [the hundreds of monks] fill the hall, hushed as though water had been sprinkled.　　水を打つ a metaphor for absolute calm like that after watering a summer garden.　　糧を両国に費やして having spent funds in both countries. 糧 literally means provisions.　　朝寄に反く to betray the imperial court's expectations. 〜に反く literally means "to go against."　　きれぎれに in bits; in fragments.

94. 心を充たしてくるものがあった there was something that began to fill his heart.　　長い歳月の翳のような妙に空漠とした感慨 an oddly vacant emotion, like the shadow of long months and years. 空漠 means vast emptiness, boundlessness.　　そうした感慨に浸って steeped in this kind of emotion.　　仏教でいう空 といったもの something like what is called "vacuity" in Buddhism.　　何かいっ ぱい詰まっていた it [the sentiment, i.e., his heart] was somehow completely filled. 長年浴びて暮らした黄色の砂粒 the yellow sand dust that he had been under all those years.　　どろどろした黄褐色の流動体 murky, yellow-brown liquid.

東大寺に数百人の僧侶が集まり、唯識、法華両宗の宗義を行賀に聴いたのは、彼が興福寺へ入ってから一カ月目のことであった。東大寺の僧明一が、試問役を引き受けて、行賀と対坐した。

行賀は明一から何を訊かれても答えられなかった。東大寺の僧明一が、試問役を引き受けて、行賀と対坐した。

行賀は明一から何を訊かれても答えられなかった。行賀は日本の言葉を口にするのがひどく不自由だった。明一は次々に何か言った。その質問の意味は判っていたが、答えるのが不自由でもあり、億劫でもあった。そして実際に何を訊かれても満足な答ができなかった。

何刻かが過ぎた。突然烈しい声が行賀の頭上に降った。

「久しく歳月を経て、学殖膚浅！」

明一の顔が、自分の前で赤く怒気を含んでいるのを、行賀は茫然として見詰めていた。そしてその向うに何百人という僧侶が水を打ったように静かに堂内を埋めているのを見た。

「糧を両国に費して」とか「朝寄に反く」とかいう言葉がきれぎれに、自分の額を打ち、頰を打つのを、行賀は感じていた。

その時、ふと、行賀の心を充たして来るものがあった。それは長い歳月の翳のような妙に空漠とした感慨であった。そうした感慨に浸って行賀は眼をつむっていた。仏教でいう空といったものとは少し違っていた。何かいっぱい詰まっていた。それは唐土で彼が永年浴びて暮らした黄色の砂粒のようなものにも思え、揚子江のどろどろした黄褐色の流動体のようなものにも思われた。行賀は自分のい

自分の今の気持ちを誰にも言い得ないのがもどかしかった he felt impatient about not being able to convey his present feeling to anybody.　　極く自然に quite spontaneously.　　その後の消息を訊いていない仙雲のこと Sen'un, whose whereabouts he had not heard of.

95. 目の前が霞んで行くのを感じた felt things go blurry before his eyes.　　数百の法衣 several hundred people in priestly robes.　　経机 a small table on which scriptures are placed.　　円柱 round pillars.　　頭上を覆う荘厳 the Buddhist canopy that covered his (and the examiner's) head.　　今まで彼の目の前にあった一切の映像 all the images that had been before his eyes until then.　　忽ち焦点を失ってぼやけていった rapidly lost their focus and faded away.　　滂沱として in streams.　　涙が頬を伝わるに任せていた left the tears to trickle down his cheeks.

96. 検問 exam questions.　　流涙したことに対しては about Gyōga's shedding tears.　　長途一蹟、豈千里の行を妨げん how can a single stumbling in a long journey obstruct the progress of a thousand leagues? 豈 is an interrogative expression used for rhetorical questions.　　森林の枯枝なんぞ万畝の影を薄うせんや how can one dead branch in the woods pale the image [of the thick foliage spread] over ten thousand furrows? 影 means anything that is projected like light, reflection, image, form, or shadow.　　一部に好意的な批判も行われた favorable critiques were conducted in some segments [of the clerical community].　　一般には否定的な言辞が弄された in general, he was critiqued in negative terms. 言辞 means speech or rhetoric. 弄する means to play with.

97.　帰国してからいっそう衰えた体を痀瘻のように屈めて（かがめて、こごめて）bending his body, which had become even more emaciated after his return to the old country, like a hunchback; Gyōga slumped/slouched like a hunchback, his body even more emaciated after his return.　　法華経弘疏賛略 Commentaries on the Lotus Sutra.　　～の筆を執り took a brush to write ～.　　唯識僉議 Inquiries into the Mind-Only Principle [of Hossō Sect Buddhism].

98. 別当 the head priest of a large temple like Kōfukuji, Tōdaiji, and Hōryūji. 延暦二十二年 803.　　寂す to die (applied to a priest's death); 寂 attaining enlightenment.

まの気持を誰にも云い得ないのがもどかしかった。行賀はなおも眼を瞑っていた。すると、極く自然に、仲麻呂と清河の二人の姿が眼にうかんで来、その後の消息を聞いていない仙雲のことが憶い出されて来た。

九五 突然行賀は眼の前が霞んで行くのを感じた。明一の顔も、数百の法衣も、経机も、円柱も、頭上を覆う荘厳も、今まで彼の眼の前にあった一切の映像が、忽ち焦点を失ってぼやけて行った。涙は行賀の眼に溢れ、滂沱として頬を流れ落ちた。行賀は長いこと涙が頬を伝わるに任せていた。

九六 後日、行賀が明一の検問に答えられず、流涙したことに対しては、いろいろの批判が行われた。長途一躓、豈千里の行を妨げんとか、深林の枯枝、何ぞ万畝の影を薄うせんやとか、そんな言葉で一部に好意的な批判も行なわれたが、併し、一般には否定的な言辞が弄された。

九七 行賀は興福寺の一室に閉じこもったまま、人と会わず、帰国してから一層衰えた躯を、佝僂のように屈めて、机に向かい続けた。『法華経弘疏賛略』の筆を執り、『唯識僉議』四十余巻の筆を執った。

九八 清河の娘、嬉娘はその後どうしたか、彼女については何も伝わっていない。

行賀は、興福寺の別当となり、延暦二十二年七十五歳で寂した。

CORNELL EAST ASIA SERIES

Order online: www.einaudi.cornell.edu/eastasia/CEASbooks, or contact Cornell East Asia Series Distribution Center, 95 Brown Road, Box 1004, Ithaca, NY 14850, USA; toll-free: 1-877-865-2432, fax 607-255-7534, ceas@cornell.edu

This book is printed Japanese-style, with pages ordered from right to left. This is the end of the book.

SB/1-07/0.5M pb/.2M hc